Francis of Assisi

D0872619

Francis of Assisi

A Life

Chiara Frugoni

CONTINUUM • NEW YORK

1999

The Continuum Publishing Company
370 Lexington Avenue
New York, NY 10017

Translated by John Bowden from the Italian
Vita di un uomo: Francesco d'Assisi
published 1995 by Giulio Einaudi Editore s.p.a., Turin

Printed in the United States of America

Library of Congress Cataloging in Publication Data

Frugoni, Chiara, 1940—
    [Vita di un uomo, Francesco d'Assisi.   English]
    Francis of Assisi : a life / Chiara Frugoni.
        p . cm .
    Includes bibliographical references and index.
    ISBN 0–8264–1098–7
    1. Francis, of Assisi, Saint, 1182–1226.   2. Christian saints –
Italy – Assisi – Biography.   3. Assisi (Italy) – Biography. I. Title.
BX4700.F6F7913 1998
271′.302–dc21   98-24354
    [b]   CIP

Contents

To Pia,
mother and grandmother,
near a small lake

I

Childhood and Youth

'In the city of Assisi, which lies at the edge of the Spoleto valley, there was a man whose name was Francis.' That is how Thomas of Celano, the first biographer of the saint, begins his account. What might seem to us to be a beginning in the style of 'Once upon a time . . .' is meant, rather, to be a learned allusion. Thomas was a highly-educated friar who had an eye for a good beginning, so he copied from the Bible the beginning of the book of Job: 'In the land of Uz there was a man whose name was Job.'

Francis died on 4 October 1226. Thomas of Celano was charged by Pope Gregory IX to write his life with great speed: the text was to be ready for the ceremony of canonization on 16 July 1228, at which Francis was officially proclaimed a saint. The pope, together with the cardinals, after an examination of all the miracles which had taken place during Francis's life and after his death ('there is testimony, discussion, verification and approval'), came to Assisi and at the end of the solemn ceremony pronounced: 'To the praise and glory of God Almighty, Father, Son and Holy Spirit, and of the glorious Virgin Mary, the blessed apostles Peter and Paul and in honour of the glorious Roman church, we venerate on earth the blessed father Francis, to whom the Lord has given glory in heaven; having received the favourable judgment of our brothers [the cardinals] and the other prelates, we decree that his name shall be inscribed in the catalogue of saints and that his festival shall be celebrated on the anniversary of his death.'

Thomas succeeded in completing his work with only a slight delay; or perhaps, more probably, he added the second and third parts, both of which are very short, at a later stage, after going to Assisi for the solemn festival at which Francis was canonized.

Our biographer introduces Francis when he was about twenty-five, on the eve of his conversion, because it was from that moment on that his devout admirers were interested in having more precise details. So Thomas does not give a complete biography, but only the second half, the story of a young man on the way to sainthood: immediately famous, controversial and disconcerting.

We therefore know nothing about the child and the young man. Certainly, we can glean some details which the author, or others after him, have let slip unintentionally. We come to see the young man of Assisi through a number of features, certain choices and mental attitudes characteristic of the adult saint. However, for these first years, we must at any rate use a reasonable degree of imagination. Still, let us begin with firm information.

We come to know from the *Legend of the Three Companions*, i.e. Angelo, Rufino and Leo, some of Francis's dearest friends (in the Middle Ages, 'legend' is to be taken in the literal sense, namely a writing intended to be read), that Francis was born while his father, a cloth merchant, was in France and that his mother had given him the name of John. However, when his father returned he had begun to call his son 'Francis', in other words 'the Frenchman'. This nickname evidently caught on, and the son allowed himself to be called by it even as an adult. That could be the first sign of a provocative and self-confident attitude on the part of Francis, aware of being destined to stand out and distinguish himself from other young men of his age, so that he was quite happy with the nickname.

There is uncertainty, too, over the name of Francis's mother: was it Pica or Giovanna? Only late and somewhat uncertain sources tell us that she was of the nobility and came from France. Her husband, Pietro di Bernadone, could have wanted to recall his wife's native country as a gesture of affection by choosing his son's name; and if French was Francis's mother tongue, that would explain why he so loved speaking in that language. It is a good explanation for a name which was still very rare at that time – 'singular and unusual', notes Thomas of Celano. But there is no solid basis for it, even if the cinema directors who have often told the story of Francis have preferred it. Others have imagined that Francis's father wanted this name to be an omen of a rich and prosperous future for his son, commemorating the successful business deal that he had just concluded in France when his son saw the light of day. Or one might think that Pietro had an inferiority complex about noblemen of an ancient line, and therefore wanted to make his son stand out by giving him a singular name, unprecedented in the family of just a rich merchant.

However, it could also be that Francis was not given this name until he was an adult, because of the enthusiasm with which he read the *chansons de geste*, the romances about Arthur and his knights of the Round Table, which could only have been available in French at that time. These stories exalted the valour of the combatants, their disinterested love of fair ladies, their loyalty, generosity and courtesy, all virtues which ideally were those of the noblemen and knights of that time. As we shall see, they made a deep and lasting impression on the young Francis. On reading them he must soon have felt stifled in the shop filled to overflowing with fabrics, and have found the plans of his father and his brother Angelo, obsessed with accounts and profits, ridiculous. Outside little Assisi, for him there were vast shady forests full of adventures, castles inhabited by kings and queens, and above all wandering knights, free to pursue their dreams.

As a child, Francis was sent to a school near his home, attached to the church of San Giorgio, the church where, some decades later, he was provisionally to be buried. Today the Chapel of the Blessed Sacrament in the church of Santa Chiara stands in its place.

The Psalter, the collection of psalms in Latin, which the children learned by heart, was used as a reading book. Learning to read under the very strict direction of the teacher – always with cane in hand – meant both learning another language, Latin, and beginning to receive religious instruction. Francis will have played on the narrow pavement in front of the church. At that time children and adults in fact lived much of their lives in the street, since the houses were small, squeezed within the surrounding walls which made space both precious and rare.

It must have been good to go out into the open air like this and to enjoy the panorama around Assisi even without being aware of it. In the summer the green fields, the woods and the olive trees were mixed with areas of ripe corn, and coloured patches of flowers. The powerful sound of bells, marking the times of prayer and work, filled the air and drowned human voices and shouts. The town criers would pass through from time to time, to announce to their trumpets the decisions of the authorities. Sometimes acrobats and jugglers gave a show, to the sound of fifes, viols and tambourines. These were not the only noises of the city; the grinding of the cartwheels, the rapid and rhythmic clip-clop of horses' hooves striking the pavements, were mixed with the cries of a host of animals: geese, chickens, sheep, goats, pigs and cows. In the eyes of a child, horses are gigantic animals, which is why it is so good to be able to master them. Francis watched them pass, ridden by noblemen dressed in precious and colourful clothes, and his imagination transformed them into heroes and paladins. He too will have galloped on a broomstick, using it as a hobby-horse. Perhaps he even had a horse on wheels, to play at jousting; and when he said his prayers in the evening perhaps he asked God not to make him a better person but to give him a magnificent horse, a real one.

Francis was born around 1181 or 1182. What the sources tell us is the date of his conversion, and even then they do so only approximately. We have to use it to calculate the date of his birth. Twenty years earlier, in 1160, the emperor Frederick I, the famous Barbarossa, knowing that he could not completely trust his uncle, Guelph VI of Bavaria, Duke of Spoleto and Tuscany, had decided to remove Assisi and the surrounding countryside from his control, since it was of great strategic importance. In fact the city was at a point where the duchy extended towards the neighbouring city of Perugia, which was protected by the church. A county was detached and entrusted to the city of Assisi itself, which thus found itself able to enjoy autonomy within the duchy of Spoleto and subsequently succeeded in laying the foundations of communal institutions. However, in Assisi the empire remained a visible and threatening presence: Barbarossa himself stayed within the powerful walls of the great fortress which dominates the city and which was called La Rocca after the rock on which it stood, as we know from three documents written between 1177 and 1186.

We need not dwell on the continual struggles over authority and rights between the Suevian emperors, the Italian communes which were coming into being and gaining strength at that time, and the papacy, which from Innocent III (elected pope in 1198, died in 1216) onwards had launched an energetic political campaign to regain the church's lands and liberties.

With the unexpected death of Henry VI, Barbarossa's son, in 1197, imperial power in central Italy crumbled. In Assisi there was a desire to overthrow it, and in 1198 La Rocca, the base of the German garrison, was attacked and destroyed. The tensions between the social components of the rising commune also reached breaking point. The *homines populi*, the ordinary people, and the new class of bourgeois merchants, rebelled against the *boni homines*, the 'well-born', knights who were descended from the old feudal nobility. These latter, probably in the service of the emperor and thus of his party, had fortified dwellings within the city and lands and castles in the neighbouring countryside. Some of the *boni homines* were killed, and others put to flight, forced to take refuge in their castles in the country, while their tall houses in Assisi were destroyed and burned down. At the same time, the defence of the city was organized and ramparts were rapidly built around it. The young Francis, then aged seventeen, could already have fought on the side of the people and thus have had real experience – no longer just in coloured miniatures – of the violence and horror of wounds and mutilations; he may have witnessed the deaths of friends, children, men and women from his native Assisi. But in these circumstances he may also have learned to costruct walls and buildings, gaining the manual skill and techniques which he made use of later when in the first days after his conversion he devoted himself to restoring ruined churches and chapels.

Because of these struggles, certain noble families took refuge in the enemy city of Perugia, which out of hatred of Assisi welcomed them with open arms: these families included the family of Clare, the future saint. The conflict extended beyond the limits of the city and became a war between Assisi and Perugia. The battle of 1203, fought at Ponte San Giovanni on the Tiber, went badly for the people of Assisi and for Francis: captured along with a large number of his fellow-citizens, he ended up in enemy prisons, where he remained for more than a year. However, 'because of his distinguished bearing, he was put among the nobles'.

While Francis had learned to bear arms, to fight on foot and on horseback, he could not devote all his time to these activities, unlike the young noblemen of Assisi, whose principal occupation it was. He had to work at the shop in order to become a good merchant. But he aspired to a change of life and social class, through the merits achieved by fighting in battle and – why not? – through marriage to a young woman of noble lineage. The *Legend of the Three Companions* tells us:

Francis grew up quick and clever, and he followed in his father's footsteps by becoming a merchant. In business, however, he was very different from Pietro, being far more high-spirited and open-handed. He was also intent on games and songs; and day and night he roamed about the city of Assisi with companions of his own age. He was a spendthrift, and all that he earned went into eating and carousing with his friends. For this his parents often remonstrated with him, saying that in squandering such large sums on himself and others, his style of living made him appear not so much their son as the son of some great prince. However, being rich and loving him tenderly, they allowed him free rein in order to avoid dis-pleasing him . . . In all things Francis was lavish, and he spent much more on his clothes than was warranted by

his social position. He would use only the finest
materials; but sometimes his vanity took on an eccentric
turn, and then he would insist on the richest cloth and the
commonest being sewn together in the same garment.

When his mother heard the comments of her astonished
neighbours, amazed at such prodigality, she defended him,
albeit with some annoyance, since he was her favourite son.

Courtesy and liberality, the virtues *par excellence* of the
aristocracy, are the values which Francis planned to culti-
vate and take as a model, adopting the ideology of chivalry.
These were virtues which did not belong to him by birth.
However,

> He was naturally courteous in manner and speech. The
> words came spontaneously from his heart, and he deter-
> mined never to say a rude or unseemly word to anyone.
> Although a gregarious and worldly youth, he would not
> answer if anyone addressed him with bad language. This
> caused his fame to spread throughout the entire province,
> and many who knew him said that he would do great
> things.

Furthermore, although he was a merchant, he liked to
spend without counting the cost. He gave readily and
generously to the poor. At this phase in his life, Francis was
not moved by compassion for the weakest, but by the social
code of his noble friends, which he observed scrupulously to
the letter, as if it was a lesson to be learned by heart.

> One day, when he was in the shop selling cloth, a beggar
> came in and asked for alms for the love of God; but
> Francis was so intent on the business of making money
> that he gave nothing to the poor man. Then, enlightened
> by divine grace, he accused himself harshly, saying, 'If

that beggar had made his request in the name of some great prince, you would surely have given him what he asked for: how much more so you should have done it when he begged in the name of the King of kings and Lord of all.'

In a great many *chansons de geste*, the catechism of laymen of high lineage, Francis would have read that one must practise 'largesse', namely liberality and generosity, or follow advice like that given to the young Fromont, the son of the duke, in the thirteenth-century romance *Garin le Lorrain*. 'Now you must strike with the spear and honour the gentle knights. Give coats of sheep's fleeces and of hides to the poor. There is one truly great thing which I ask of you: it is by a gift that a man of valour gains high esteem.'

Raoul de Houdenc's *Roman des ailes*, composed between 1170 and 1230, explains how, in order to fly high, 'prowess' must provide itself with two wings, 'liberality' and 'courtesy'.

During the long crisis which preceded his conversion, Francis made a pilgrimage to Rome. When he entered St Peter's, he thought the alms given to the prince of the apostles too modest, nothing but small change. He said to himself that the prince of the apostles was 'due the greatest honour'. He then impetuously threw a fistful of silver through a grating in the altar, which, clattering noisily, provoked the amazement of the bystanders. Here was yet another extravagant gesture to arouse admiration, even if here it had a religious basis. But equally present is the idea that a saint must be honoured because he is a great prince. This was precisely Francis's ideal, for which his parents constantly reproved him.

The young merchant knew how to transform the nobility of manners into a nobility of rank, though he always suffered because of his origins, which were an indelible mark. At the end of his life, sick and covered with sores, he got down from the donkey on which he was riding, having guessed the thoughts of the companion who was following him on foot: 'Brother, it is neither just nor fitting that I should ride on horseback when you are walking on foot, for in the world you were *more noble* and richer than me.' Even the ostentation of his clothing, imitating the fashion of the *miparti*, that garment of precious cloth divided into two halves of different colours, had an air of arrogance and provocation. For his clothes, Francis had a precious fabric and a coarser, cheap one sewn together; it was a way of distancing himself from family customs, without denying them completely. This eccentricity persisted a long time – later, when at the head of a community, he prescribed that the habits of the brothers should be decorated with all kinds of bits and pieces. He fastened a fox's pelt to his own habit, thus indicating on *the outside* the presence of the twin fur sewn inside to ease the pain of his skin disease.

In prison in Perugia he showed himself gentle and affable towards a *miles*, i.e. a knight, but this man was distant and insulting: he will have been one of the nobles from the countryside or from an allied city who had been summoned by the commune of Assisi for the disastrous battle of Ponte San Giovanni. This man will have had at least two reasons to complain: finding himself in prison, and moreover in such inferior company, merchants and rich artisans, not even his equals! At all events, this small episode too is indicative of Francis's choices; he carefully selected the people with whom he became friends. While his prison companions became downhearted and sad, Francis, cheerful and jovial by nature, far from abandoning himself to depression, seemed almost to enjoy being in such a situation. His demeanour infuriated one of the prisoners, who, by all the evidence, could no longer bear to spend his time in so much discomfort. He told Francis that he was a fool to look happy in prison. Francis then replied to him in a vibrant tone: 'What do you think I shall become in life? I shall be honoured by the whole world!'

Joy is also a characteristic of Francis's: the *Legend of the Three Companions* presents it as an element in his character. It is hard to judge: though it may indeed have been an innate quality, Francis certainly cultivated it at the cost of vigilant self-control, resolved to sublimate all pain and suffering of body and spirit by an unquenchable inner strength. When he thought he would still become a prince, he made trial of the virtues of courage and physical endurance, forged by bearing arms, through long acclimatization to the dangers and pains of wounds. When he firmly decided to follow the example of Christ, he resorted to the virtues of serene patience and joyful obedience: patience which allowed him to tolerate the will of others, and obedience, which dominates and tames ambition and that pride which consists in knowing oneself to be better than others.

However, for the moment, his long detention did not succeed in stifling the dreams of the young man of twenty, who had decided to make his way by the point of his sword. After a whole year, the gate of the prison in Perugia finally opened. Francis and his companions returned to Assisi, perhaps as result of the peace charter established in 1203. This pact also entailed the return to the city of the *boni homines*, and contained clauses which bore heavily on the men of the 'people'. They found themselves forced to rebuild the tall houses of the exiles, and still had to offer *hominitia*, i.e. to remain subject to a series of levies without having control of their own goods. All in all, this was a return to the situation of before 1198.

The Francis whom his family once again embraced was seriously ill: while his will may have resisted the terrible experience of Perugia, his fragile constitution had been sorely tried. For a long period Francis was a poor invalid.

Then little by little he recovered: leaning on a stick, he took several steps inside his house. Then, somewhat strengthened, he went out. Moving with great difficulty and somewhat embarrassed, he was led to reflect: 'He began to look about at the surrounding landscape with great interest. But the beauty of the fields, the pleasantness of the vine-yards, and what ever else was beautiful to look upon, could stir in him no light. He wondered therefore at the sudden change that had come over him, and those who took delight in such things he considered very foolish.' Thomas of Celano makes this long period of inactivity coincide with the beginning of a profound crisis, full of ruminations, decisions taken and suddenly abandoned. He suggests that this reaction was not just the result of the transitory apathy of a convalescent but the first fruits of a total inner reversal, willed by heaven. From the moment that he discovered that what he saw around him did not attract him in the least, Francis 'began to despise himself and to hold in some contempt the things he had admired and loved before. But not fully or truly, for he was not yet freed from the cords of vanity nor had he yet shaken off from his neck the yoke of evil servitude.' The biographer then embarks on a long commentary moralizing on the power of vices, which by repetition become second nature. Thomas forces his interpretation a bit, but he is acute enough to make the surrounding contryside an echo of Francis's unhappiness, thus painting a perfectly coherent psychological portrait. We almost get the impression that it is Francis who is inventing the countryside, through the capacity he has to see it and to love it. Later, now already living with his brothers, he advised the gardener brother: 'Do not plant it all with vegetables, but leave a bit of ground free so that there will be wild plants which in their time produce our sisters the flowers.' He even used to say that the brother gardener should reserve a place in a corner of the garden where he could put all kinds of aromatic herbs and flowering plants. Once they blossomed, by their beauty they would invite anyone who looked upon them to praise God.

In prison, Francis had wanted to see his city of Assisi, his friends, his parents and his family again. But now all this had become alien to him and a matter of indifference. Above all he seemed no longer to have an aim in life. To devote all his energy to earning money like his father or his brother Angelo no longer meant anything to him, and would not be enough to fill his life. To gain glory in combat – was this still possible, now that he had noted how fragile his constitution was? Would it not be better to be patient, to hope that his enjoyment of former diversions would return, to regain strength, to begin to gallop again and to practise bearing arms?

These are the kind of thoughts that we attribute to the convalescent Francis. The *Legend of the Three Companions* tells only that some years passed after his return to Assisi before there was any great occasion to realize his dreams of glory. The account continues: 'A certain nobleman of the city of Assisi was preparing himself in no mean way with military arms, and, puffed up by a gust of vainglory, vowed that he would go to Apulia to increase his wealth and fame.' Here it must be recalled that in southern Italy Pope Innocent III was facing the imperial troops led by Markwald of Anweiler. Two particularly delicate and important matters were at stake: the recovery of the patrimony of the church and the guardianship of the young son of Henry VI, the future emperor Frederick II. At that time the pontiff had thought that he could rely on a skilful man of arms, Gualtier of Brienne. Gualtier, who had married the daughter of Tancred of Lecce, wanted to obtain the great fiefs of Puglia; he was happy to assemble in a mercenary army all those who wanted to take part in the expedition; the 'nobleman of Assisi' mentioned in the *Legend of the Three Companions* was one of their number.

When informed of the enterprise, Francis immediately decided to join his fellow-citizen: 'In the hope of being made a knight by the noble count, he prepared magnificent equipment; and, though his fellow citizen was a nobleman, Francis was by far the more extravagant of the two.' That is how the knights behaved in romances: in Chrétien de Troyes' *Cligés*, the son of the emperor of Greece takes leave of his father, saying: 'I wish to have an abundance of your gold and silver, and such companions from among your men as I shall choose, for I wish to leave your empire and present my service to the king who rules Britain so that he may make me a knight.' Reluctantly his father grants him permission, but not without adding some urgent advice: 'Dear son, since I see you striving for glory, I must not fail to do what pleases you. You may fill two boats with gold and silver from my treasury. But you must always show largesse, courtesy, and good manners . . . to give and to spend lavishly.'

Francis threw himself body and soul into making preparations. Eager to set out, one day he had a dream: someone called him by name and led him into a splendid palace, where there was a very beautiful lady; the palace was full of glittering coats of mail, shining bucklers and all the weapons and armour of warriors. Francis, Thomas of Celano remarks, was all the more amazed, since at home he was accustomed to see only rolls of cloth. Delighted, full of happiness and mute admiration, he finally decided to ask to whom this shining armour and marvellous palace belonged. He was told that the palace was for him – as also was the lady – and his knights. When he woke up, full of enthusiasm, he was certain that this dream was an excellent omen and that an exceptional destiny awaited him. To those who were amazed to see him so cheerful and radiant he replied: 'I know that I shall become a great prince.' Without waiting any longer, he decided to leave for Puglia immediately. Of course, intent on his worldly projects, he did not think for a moment that the vision could have been sent to him by God – as the *Legend of the Three Companions* reports – and that it therefore meant something very different. The day before this dream of the palace and its arms, when they were eagerly waiting to set off, Francis had given all his most expensive new clothes prepared for the occasion, which were both luxurious and striking, to a poor knight. And the *Three Companions*, which by all the evidence truly knew Francis (and who had devised the concept of the dream as a 'residue of the day') again notes that it was certainly this gift which had brought on the dream.

The young merchant was thinking of great enterprises. He saw himself already a knight and therefore behaved in keeping with this future which he longed for so much; so he deigned, generously, to clothe the knight who had fallen on hard times, as though this knight had a lower social rank than he did.

'My dear son,' again the father in the *Cligés* advises, 'believe me when I tell you that largesse is the queen and lady who brightens all virtues, as is not at all difficult to prove. Where could one find a man who, no matter how powerful and rich, who would not be reproached if he were miserly? . . . Largesse alone makes a worthy man, not high birth, courtesy, wisdom, power, beauty, gentility, riches, strength, chivalry, boldness, power, beauty, or any other gift.'

So Francis's gift is very much in line with his former reflections, when, regretting that he had driven a poor man from the shop, he blamed himself for not living up to the image of the perfect knight which he was taking pains to imitate. So we begin to understand that such surprising signs of courtesy and nobility of spirit are presages of holiness.

But Francis did not know that, and for the moment he was happy to arouse admiration. The dream met with all his desires, and granted him even more than he had ever dared consciously to hope for: he saw himself not only as a knight but as a prince, not just as a companion equal to other knights, but as their leader. And thanks to the great merits he had acquired in war he believed that he had already married a very beautiful lady who was only awaiting his return.

Francis left, but did not get very far. At Spoleto he began to feel unwell. Evidently he was very preoccupied with the long journey ahead of him. He decided to rest. In his drowsing it seemed to him that someone was asking him where he thought that he was going. Having learned his destination, this person said to him: 'Who do you think can best reward you, the master or his servant?'

'The master.'

'Then why are you leaving the master for the servant, the rich lord for the poor man?'

'O Lord, what do you wish me to do?'

'Return to your own place, and you will be told what to do. You must interpret your vision in a different sense.'

We should note the perspective of the vassal which was typical of Francis, who saw himself as a knight in the service of his lord: for him God was a great prince. Fully awake, he reflected at length. If the first dream had made him almost crazy with joy, this new vision 'forced him to recollect himself'. He did not sleep a wink all night, continuing to think about what he should do. At dawn his decision had been made: he mounted his horse and returned to Assisi. He totally changed all his plans, and had nothing more to do with the expedition to Puglia. Now he wanted only to know and follow the will of God.

2

The Parting

Francis returned to Assisi. In the eyes of his family and his friends this sudden return must have appeared a failure. Where was all the warlike prowess which would have made the merchant a knight? Vanished, like a soap bubble.

Perhaps it was precisely in order to revive his tarnished image, to put an end to indiscreet questions and to hide his inner disquiet, that Francis joined in more and more festivities with his friends. During one of these evenings he was elected 'king of the banquet' and was given no less than a sceptre: in reality this was just a stick, but the role of the *rex convivii*, the king of the feast, was already known in Roman antiquity. According to the custom in Assisi, as king he was expected to decide who was to take on the expense of the banquet and to fix the cost. His friends, knowing Francis's lavishness, were certain that the king himself would always pay for a sumptuous banquet. And that is what happened. So the 'monarch' continued to reign for a long time. One evening after the feast, the company, singing noisily, went through the quiet and dark streets of Assisi. During this nocturnal walk Francis, absorbed in his thoughts, became separated from his companions. He suddenly stopped, by divine will. His friends asked him: 'What were you thinking of that you forgot to follow us? Did you plan to take a woman?' And Francis, with one of the exaggerated expressions which he affected, immediately replied: 'Yes, I stood thinking of taking a bride more noble, more rich and more beautiful than any that you have ever seen!'

Everyone began to laugh, and the matter ended there. The *Legend of the Three Companions* adds that this reply of Francis's was inspired by God, since it is true that later he espoused the religious life: such a commentary is inevitable in the life of a saint. But the repartee is very much in keeping with the ambitions of the dissatisfied merchant. His chief desire was to marry a noble wife: he envisaged leaving his rank by marriage, by choosing a wife who would allow him to rise in social class. Perhaps Francis, immobile, absorbed, was still thinking of the palace and the arms, the mysterious words of the dream of Spoleto. The course of his conversion was long and tortuous. The *Legend* notes the slowness and difficulty with which old habits were abandoned.

The future saint continued to work at the shop, but he became more pious: he gave more alms, and even went so far as to give away his shirt if he found himself without money. He also gave poor priests the objects they needed to adorn their churches. If formerly he had been eager to join his friends, introducing his parents in the middle of the feast, now he stayed at home. In the absence of his father, of whom he had a great fear, Francis would put more bread on the table than there were people around it – at that time bread served as plates – so that there would be more left over to distribute to the needy. His mother, whose favourite he was, just smiled and let it happen. It is probable that as well as being a cloth merchant, his father, Pietro di Bernadone, was a money-lender.

Francis must have been very struck by the changes of fortune brought about by the frenetic movement of money. Alongside the old poor (the peasants, the day labourers, the sick and single persons), new poor were constantly being created: we might remember the knight to whom Francis had given all his equipment. As well as the terrible social inequalities of birth there were constantly yet others. There were so many ways of becoming poor: one had only to fail to repay a sum of money in time; it only took a riot, a house burned down in one of the frequent fires (at that time cities contained many wooden buildings). A broken arm, the slightest physical infirmity – at that time there were no x-rays or plasters – which prevented someone from working flung him into the category of the cripples who asked for charity. As well as the toiling citizens, a ragged and lurid crowd of beggars wandered through the streets of Assisi; Francis came upon them every day, with a mixture of repulsion and compassion. Alongside them wandered the crazy and the mad, brusquely nicknamed the 'possessed', who were also forced to swell the ranks of the needy.

Francis knew yet other horrors which he tried to escape, not always with success. Outside Assisi, two leper colonies (Santa Maria Maddalena and San Salvatore) lodged men and women of repugnant appearance who were shunned by all: it was thought that the lepers had been struck with their disease as a divine punishment, for the sins that they had committed, or because they had been conceived in sin. Because of this, as they walked they had to sound clappers to allow healthy people to get out of the way. On his solitary excursions, Francis sought to keep his distance from where they lived; he spurred on his horse so that he would not see them, turning its head away from them.

During the long period of uncertainty and crisis in which he found himself plunged, Francis looked for help. He confided in a friend – unfortunately we do not know his name – and often asked advice from Guido, bishop of Assisi. He withdrew into a cave to pray and meditate, uncertain of what to do. He was not yet ready completely to forget his past. He loved life, ease, the luxury in which he lived. He knew that his health was fragile, that he needed a degree of comfort. And then, he was now a full-grown man. He was approaching twenty-five, the age at which, if his father allowed him to leave his apprenticeship, he could become a merchant on his own account.

In the cave where he was gathering his thoughts, he obsessively recalled 'a woman of Assisi, humpbacked and deformed': that is what he would become, bent and twisted, if he continued with his intentions. He could not accept physical degradation: he was still too fond of himself.

What a long course still Francis had to cover before he could think of poverty as an idealized friend, 'Lady Poverty'!

On the pilgrimage to Rome mentioned earlier, the young merchant had distributed arms more than generously. But he had also tried to play the poor man by exchanging his clothes for some hours with those of a beggar. Then he had sat on the steps of St Peter's, asking for alms, in French, amongst the other beggars.

Francis looked wretched, but his heart was certainly not. That is the reason why he begged and asked for charity not in his own tongue, but in French. He chose to speak in this language, different from that to which he was accustomed – we shall find some more examples later – only on very particular occasions. Francis had recourse to the language of the paladins and the knights when he needed their model to get over fear and shame in the name of generosity, loyalty and disinterested courage.

Then one day, when he was riding in the streets of Assisi, he met a leper. He forced himself to get down from his horse and give the wretched man some money; he kissed his hand and allowed the leper to embrace him. Some days later, he decided to meet the lepers again. He collected a large sum of money and went to their hospice, once again kissed their hands, covered with sores, gave them alms and allowed himself to be embraced.

This was a radical change. Twenty years later, on the verge of dying, he began his *Testament* by summing up, in a few very intense words, this experience which marked the dawn of a new life:

> This is how God inspired me, Brother Francis, to embark upon a life of penance. When I was in sin, the sight of lepers nauseated me beyond measure; but then God himself led me into their company, and I had pity on them. When I had once become acquainted with them, what had previously nauseated me became a source of spiritual and physical consolation for me. After that I did not wait long before leaving the world.

Who knows whether in these very fine words there is not a distant echo of something that Francis read in his youth? One thinks in particular of a passage from the romance *Cligés* by Chrétien de Troyes, in which the magician Thessala says to Fenice, who is in love with Cligés: 'All sorts of pain are always horrible and cruel, except the pain of love alone. But love turns its bitterness into sweetness.' Can we not also think that Francis felt justified in advance for the repulsion which he felt when confronting lepers on reading, in Béroult's *Tristan*, the punishment imagined by them quite specifically for Yseut, the adulterous wife of King Mark?

> There was a leper in Lantyan, his name was Ivain and he was terribly infirm. He had hurried up to see what was going on. He had a good hundred companions with him, carrying their sticks and crutches. You never saw people

so ugly or hunched or deformed. Each was holding his clapper. Ivain called hoarsely to the king: 'Sire, you wish to do justice by burning your wife like this. It is a harsh punishment but, if ever I knew anything, it will not last long. That great fire will soon burn her and the wind will scatter her ashes. The fire will subside and all that is left of her punishment will be cinders. That is the punishment you are going to give her. But, if you would listen to me, I could tell you of a way to punish her so that she would rather have been put to death than be still living in dishonour. Anyone who came to hear of this would think the more of you. King, would you like to do this?' The king listened and said: 'If you can tell me, without a trick, how she may live and be dishonoured, I shall be grateful to you. Take something of mine, if you wish. No manner of death is so grim and horrible that I shall not love for ever, by God the king, that man who today can choose the worst for her!' Ivain answered: 'I can tell you quickly what I have in mind. Look, here I have a hundred companions. Give Yseut to us and we will possess her in common. No woman ever had a worse end. Sire, there is such lust in us that no woman on earth could tolerate intercourse with us for a single day. The very clothes stick to our bodies. With you she used to be honoured and happily clad in blue and grey furs. She learned of good wines in your marble halls. If you give her to us lepers, when she sees our low hovels and looks at our dishes and has to sleep with us – in place of your fine meals, sire, she will have the pieces of food and crumbs that are left for us at the gates – then, by the Lord who dwells above, when she sees our court and all its discomforts she would rather be dead than alive. The snake Yseut will know then that she has been wicked! She would rather have been burnt.' The king listened to him, stood up and said nothing for a long while. He had heard what Ivain had said. He ran to Yseut and took her by the hand. Yseut cried out: 'Sire, mercy! Burn me here instead of giving me to them!' The king handed her over to the lepers and a good hundred crowded around her. Everyone who heard the noise and the shouting took pity on her. But whoever might be sorrowful, Ivain was happy. He led Yseut away along the sandy path.

Francis does not offer a political response to social injustices, to the problem of evil in the world. He has no plans for effective and concrete changes; he does not plan either struggles or rebellions. He responds in faith, with a total and impetuous adherence, when he succeeds in penetrating to the depths of the sacrifice of Christ. Let us try to follow his train of thought. God, the Most High, master of the universe, of all creation, has sacrificed his only beloved Son so as not to allow his own creature, this human being who cannot but sin, to rush to his doom. And if the Christ who is God has come on earth, moved by an immense love, if he has made himself poor and a pilgrim, has endured heat and cold, betrayal and abandonment by his friends, if he has gone so far as to give his life on the cross to offer salvation again to humanity, to open up for it the eternal joy of paradise, what else is there for human beings to do than to follow, as far as they can, in the footsteps of the Saviour, of the gospel; to respond to the divine love by their poor human love, seeking to love one another as brothers? And who better than the poor man, the one who is abandoned, because he renews in his suffering the earthly experience of Christ? He can understand better the ardent divine love and accept anguish and pain with gratitude, submitting like Christ to the will of the Father. The *Little Flowers of St Francis*, a marvellous collection in the vernacular of the 'miracles and pious examples' of the life of Francis, dating from the last quarter of the fourteenth century, attributed to him these words as a definition of the virtue of perfect joy:

> Above all the graces and gifts of the Holy Spirit which Christ granted to his friends is that of conquering oneself, and willingly for love of Christ enduring tribulations, injuries, insults and hurts: we must not boast in any of the other gifts of God, which are not ours but God's, as the apostle says: 'What do you have that you do not have from God? And if you have it from him, why do you glory as though you had it from yourselves?' (Paul, in I Corinthians 4.7). But we can glory in the cross of tribulations and afflictions, as the apostle says (again Paul, in Galatians 6.14): 'I will not glory except in the cross of our saviour Jesus Christ.'

'After that, I did not wait long before leaving the world': in this short phrase Francis sums up the moments which saw him irresolute, tied to his family, his milieu, fearing the reaction of his father, anxious, believing that he had at last found a way, only to perceive that this was still a false start.

One day he entered the little church of San Damiano. He began to pray intensely before a crucifix painted on wood. (The crucifix has come down to us and is now preserved in the church of Santa Chiara.) The Redeemer, who, in keeping with the iconography of the triumphant Christ, bears no trace of physical suffering, fixes the observer with a serene sweetness. Francis believed that the cross was truly addressing him and saying to him: 'Francis, do not you see how my house is falling into ruin? Go and repair it for me!' Once more, the symbolic meaning of the words escaped him: he thought that he had to save the material building from ruin and was far from imagining the task which awaited him: to save the spiritual building, the church. He went out quite content; it seemed to him that his life at last had a goal. It had not been fear of damnation which robbed him of peace, but the void which he saw gaping before him. Now he knew what he had to do; the mysterious words of the dream in Spoleto began to become clear: he could also see for the first time the one who was calling him and hear his name being pronounced. So that was the order that he was waiting for.

His first resolution was to give money to the priest who was sitting in front of the church: Francis wanted a lamp always to burn in front of the crucifix and he promised to give more money for this purpose when it was needed. Some time later he loaded a horse with bales of precious fabrics, went to Foligno and sold it all, horse included. He returned to San Damiano on foot, free and light. He wanted to give his purse full of money to the priest, who had only meagre resources, and asked at the same time to be allowed to live with him. The poor man heard the story of Francis's conversion, astonished and incredulous. But he would not accept the money at any price, fearing the all too foreseeable reaction of Pietro di Bernadone. In the end, after many hesitations, he agreed to allow the young man to live with him.

Francis then flung the money on the outside window sill of a church. Perhaps he had seen a picture in the church of St Nicolas in Assisi, which he often entered, of one of the most famous episodes from the life of this saint. When Nicolas was still young, rich and handsome, he had learned that an old wretch was planning to sell his three daughters into prostitution to get something to live on. The saint had then thrown three golden balls at the window of the poor house as a dowry for the three girls and to save their honour. (St Nicolas, who is usually represented as a venerable bishop with white hair, always holds three golden balls in his hand as a souvenir of this episode from his generous youth.)

Francis's prolonged absence began to concern his father seriously. When Pietro discovered where his son was living, he felt sorrow, anger and bitterness. Had he been wise to invest so much money in him? And then, what would he do in life? To think that he had hoped that his 'Francesino' would become a rich merchant, richer than he and perhaps, who knows, a knight. And instead of that he had become a fool and a vagabond.

Disconcerted by this incredible *volte-face*, Pietro called on friends and neighbours to help him get back his rebellious son. But Francis had foreseen his father's anger and took refuge in a secret cave which had been prepared for this eventuality. He will probably have been warned by someone at home – his mother? – the person who during the month of his previous voluntary captivity in the cave had brought him food every day.

This was a very harsh period: the future saint hesitated to break definitively with his family, to leave everything, all that he loved most, to follow a course on which he felt irresistibly drawn, but which seemed to him to be uncertain. What if he was deceived, if he came to regret it, if he discovered that it was all a mistake? He wept, prayed and fasted, alternating between anxiety and the highest of hopes. The day came when he felt brave enough to come out and confront his father. On the road which led to his home the people whom he met looked at him in astonishment; they barely recognized him, so much had he changed. He was thin and pale from fasting, dirty. They thought that he had gone mad and began to throw stones and handfuls of mud at him, as though he were crazy, especially the children. The rumour ran through the squares and streets of Assisi that Francis had returned. The noise reached his father's ears. When he realized that it was his son who was the laughing-stock of the moment he rushed outside, seized with a blind fury, driven on by deep sorrow, desperate. He had to put an end to this humiliation. Wasn't he, too, the target of the handfuls of mud? He pushed Francis into the house, showering blows on him, and kept him shut up for days and days in a dark little room, resolved to put an end to his whims. During one of Pietro's absences his wife did not obey his instructions: after doing all she could to convince Francis, she was seized with pity, opened the door and let her beloved son go. When her husband returned she had to face his wrath: the man felt cheated and betrayed.

If this really was a definitive rebellion, at least Francis should repay what he had unduly benefitted from: the anger of the merchant, wrongly robbed of his goods, exacerbated the sorrow of the father. Pietro decided to summon his son before the consuls: he rushed to the palace of the commune and gave his reasons. The consuls sent a herald to Francis with an order to appear before them, but Francis responded with a very skilful manoeuvre. Had he already asked the bishop's advice? He forestalled his father: he claimed to be living as a penitent and therefore no longer to be subject to the jurisdiction of the commune, but to that of the church. The consuls, to avoid trouble, judged the reply satisfactory. The father would not accept defeat and ran to the bishop, who had Francis called: this time the rebel obeyed.

Faced with father and son, the bishop turned to his protégé, who meanwhile had had the good idea of bringing all the money he still had. The prelate exhorted him: 'Your father is highly incensed and greatly scandalized by your conduct. If therefore you wish to serve God, you must first of all return him his money, which indeed may have been dishonestly acquired. God would not wish you to use it for restoring the church.' Francis acquiesced: he gave back everything. He went into a neighbouring room, stripped, and returned, naked, to his father and all those present, holding his clothes in his hands with the money on top of them. Imagine the crowd of friends and neighbours who surveyed the scene, holding their breath as Francis said: 'Listen all of you and mark my words. Hitherto I have called Pietro di Bernadone my father; but because I am resolved to serve God, I return to him the money on account of which he was so perturbed, and also the clothes that I wore that are his; and from now on I will say "Our Father who art in heaven", and not father Pietro Bernadone.'

Hearing these definitive words from his son, Pietro di Bernadone, burning with grief and anger, gathered up the garments and the money and rushed home, where he shut himself in. The bishop then opened his arms and covered the naked man with his cloak. This gesture, immortalized by Giotto, which forms part of all the cycles of pictures which relate the saint's life, had a deeper sense than a simple gesture of hope: it indicated Francis's irrevocable detachment, abandoning his natural family to enter the spiritual family of the church. That is how it was interpreted by the spectators of the time and that is how it is always interpreted by readers. The break was brusque and painful, and not just for Francis's father. Francis himself also suffered terribly: his magnificent commentary on the Our Father bears the traces of a profound sorrow. In all his writings Francis always emphasized the fatherly face of God, the vigilant and unfailing love for humankind which he expresses through the sacrifice of his well-beloved Son, to the point of the final salvation which time still has to unveil. In Francis's theological view the sacrifice of Christ did not coincide with his death, since it was already totally consummated on the Mount of Olives in obedience to the heavenly Father; in return, sinful man can only be ransomed by following the traces left by the great Brother, taking Christ as an example in submitting to the will of the Father. In this relationship, which is so original, there is clearly an immediate and direct indication of a yearning for a bond with the father, broken for ever, but never forgotten.

After the dramatic scene before the bishop, and when the tension which had supported him so far had slackened, Francis unexpectedly found himself alone. It was winter. He began his new life in the rigours of cold, with little clothing, no house, no family. Like his dear knights of the romances who, when they had finished one great enterprise set off again into the forest in search of adventure, Francis threw himself into the unknown. He went into a wood, singing the praises of God in French. A band of robbers suddenly rushed at him and ferociously asked who he was. 'I am the herald of the great king,' he replied. 'What is that to you?' This arrogant retort, which hardly went with his attire – Francis was in rags and tatters – , coupled with the fact that they did not get a penny from the encounter, infuriated the robbers. Francis was struck and thrown into a ditch full of snow: 'Lie there, foolish herald of God!', they said. When the robbers had gone, Francis got out of the ditch, shook the snow off his clothes and again, singing in a loud voice, resumed his way towards a monastery. This strange declaration had prompted him to play the role of the poor herald described in *Lancelot*, another romance by Chrétien de Troyes. Lancelot, exhausted, was resting after a tournament in which he had fought incognito when 'a barefooted young fellow clad only in his shirt came running up. He was a herald-at-arms who had lost his cloak and shoes gambling in the tavern, and was now barefoot with nothing to protect him from the cool air.' When he got to Lancelot, who had left the door open, and recognized him, the poor herald, full of admiration, rushed out of the house and ran off shouting: 'The one who will save you is come! You shall see what he will do! Today you will be witnesses of it.' But Francis was the herald of an invisible king; moreover, when he arrived at the monastery he was given a suspicious reception by the monks, who showed him no charity. They made him a scullion in the kitchen and treated him badly; they even refused him a drop of soup. He was cold and hungry, but no one covered him or fed him. Need, not anger, then forced him to resume his journey. He went to Gubbio, where a man who was still well disposed gave him a tunic to protect him from the bad weather.

Francis then turned his back on the organized spiritual care from which he had thought that he would find help and support. He had gone to the wrong house: his was the leper colony where he was to live, looking after and serving the unfortunate inhabitants. However, he did not forget the words of the crucifix: he restored the little church of San Damiano, then another (probably San Pietro, next to the ramparts of Assisi), and finally another, at the Portiuncula, in the plain which stretches out in front of Assisi, very near to the leper colonies of Santa Maria Maddalena and San Salvatore. Today the Portiuncula is surrounded by the church of Santa Maria degli Angeli, enormous and cold: anyone who crosses the threshold gets the painful impression that this minuscule building with blackened walls is no more than a forgotten ruin, in blatant contrast to the polished marble and the vastness of the dome which extends over it. Only a great effort of inner concentration makes it possible to imagine it as it was, lost in the middle of a thick wood, and to recall that these are the rough stones which were touched and assembled by the saint's hands, which welcomed his prayers and those of his first companions.

The sources do not agree on the order of Francis's first

actions: one might suppose that he alternated care of the sick and laborious manual work, living sometimes at the leper colony, and sometimes at San Damiano, at least while he was repairing the walls of the little church, which were on the point of falling down. He dressed like a hermit: a leather belt on top of his poor tunic, sandals, and a long staff in his hand. In the Middle Ages even more than today, given the rigidity of social divisions and the need immediately to put everyone immediately in his right place, this way of dressing functioned as a code. Francis's hermit's clothes were reassuring: moreover, restoring churches was one of the typical activities of those who led a solitary life of penance.

Francis scoured Assisi to get stones, singing the praises of God with fervour and then proclaiming like a town crier, 'Whoever gives me one stone will have one reward; two stones, two rewards; three stones a treble reward!' The passers-by listened, flabbergasted.

'Many other simple words fell from his lips and he spoke from the fervour of his heart, for he had been chosen by God to be simple and unlearned, using none of the erudite words of human wisdom,' write the *Three Companions*, who perhaps personally witnessed this unusual preaching. The people reacted in different ways: some thought that he had gone completely mad and treated him accordingly, mocking him and insulting him; but others were struck by Francis's overwhelming enthusiasm and his physical transformation. They recalled a young man with the smartest clothing, who loved to amuse himself and lead the good life with his friends, spending lavishly. And here they had before them a poor young man, thin and pale, who loftily asked for help and promised divine rewards.

The attitude was the same when, on a bitter winter's day, Francis happened to meet his brother Angelo. Francis was shivering with cold and, to mock him, Angelo said to a friend: 'Ask Francis to sell you a few pence of his sweat.' Francis replied immediately in French, not without a touch of the quarrelsome brother, 'I will sell it more dearly to my Lord'.

At this time, 'when his father saw him in this pitiful plight he was filled with sorrow, for he had loved him very dearly; he was both grieved and ashamed to see his son half dead from penance and hardships, but whenever they met, he cursed Francis.' It was not easy even for Francis to bear this, so to put an end to it, one day he went in search of a poor man. He promised him a reward and said to him: 'Come with me. When I hear my father cursing me, I shall turn to you, saying, "Father, bless me"; and then you will make the sign of the cross and bless me in his place.' The occasion arose very soon. And while blessings and curses were being exchanged, the son said to his true father: 'Do you not realize that God can give me a father whose blessing will counter your curses?' These are bitter words, and they are the last that Francis exchanged with the members of his family. From that moment on, father, mother and brothers left the scene for ever: a saint is a son only of God.

Meanwhile, the poor priest of San Damiano had become fond of this new friend whom he had welcomed into his home. He offered him some of his own food, but, recalling the refined habits of his young companion, he tried to prepare something special for him. Francis noticed this and thereupon decided that his model must be Christ, 'who was born poor, lived very poor in this world, remained poor and naked on the cross, and was buried in another's tomb'. This meant being truly poor. He had to return to Assisi and beg alms from door to door: food which had gone off so that no one wanted it any more. He went into the city and, without paying too much attention to the comments and the surprise of those who found him camped in front of their door, mixed together a large amount of scraps. 'When it came to eating the contents of the bowl, Francis' stomach turned, for he had never seen such a mess, let along tried to eat it.' He managed to overcome his disgust and then felt a great calmness: the bitter had been made sweet. However, when he knocked on the doors of friends who were engaged in play, he found it more difficult to control himself. As he heard the echoes of the familiar voices which had mingled with his at so many feasts, Francis suddenly no longer had the courage to knock, and retraced his steps. But he thought better of it, confessed his cowardice in a loud voice, went into the house, and asked, *in French*, to be given, for the love of God, some oil for the lamp of San Damiano.

At this time he was pursuing his work of restoring ruined churches. While he was carrying hods of mortar, bricks and stones, on his frail shoulders, he kept calling out in French: 'Come and help us do this work for the church of San Damiano which will become a convent for ladies whose life and fame will cause our heavenly Father to be universally glorified.' Behind these words, the Latin prose of the *Legend of the Three Companions* allows us to see a French poem and to recover the rhymes: Damien, Dames, Fame, Celestien.

The biographers then interpret Francis's call as a prophecy which is proved true at every point: was it not precisely at San Damiano that there was to be born, some years later, 'the glorious and splendid order of the Poor Ladies and holy virgins' led by Clare? But Francis was probably singing a pious adaptation of a song which he had composed himself, in which the Lady in question must have been the Madonna. With time, and because it was at San Damiano that Clare and her companions were to live later, his generalized call for someone to help him to honour and increase the renown of the Virgin and of God, the heavenly

Father, was turned into the memory of a very precise prophecy.

Francis owed his success to his very special way of addressing a crowd: he preached in simple and spontaneous language, resorting to gestures, mime, song and music. For the audience it was like watching a play, a religious comedy. Once, during a serious illness, although it was Lent, he had eaten chicken. Hardly had he recovered somewhat than he went to the gates of Assisi and asked a companion to put a cord round his neck and to drag him naked through the city, like a thief. The brother, improvising as a herald, was ordered to cry: 'Look at this glutton who without your knowing it stuffed himself with chicken!' The contrast between the words denouncing alleged hypocrisy and the sight of the poor broken body of a man whom everyone regarded as a saint aroused great emotion: the process immediately proved effective, prompting the audience to repent and to behave better.

However, Francis did not just have the skill of a great actor and a holy jester; he used words with the mastery of a famous advocate. The archdeacon and chronicler Thomas of Spalato recalls a memorable homily of Francis on the theme 'Angels, men and demons' which he gave in Bologna in 1222 in front of the town hall, 'where all the city seemed to have met'. The author notes the astonished admiration of the 'men of letters', educated people who knew Latin, when confronted with a sermon by an uneducated man who could nevertheless communicate his message in a new and convincing way. The audience thought they were listening to one of their own, brilliant and lively, and not one of the religious who were usually so boring and difficult to follow. Francis knew how to hold the attention of the crowd with a sometimes surprising casualness, interpreting for example in a Christian sense the thoughts of the lover impatient to be united with his fair lady. This is what we read in the tragic story of the *Chatelaine of Vergy:* 'There is no need to describe or to listen to the joy of the two lovers. Only the one who is awaiting that joy which love gives to loving purposes when it recompenses them for their pains may follow the story.'

And at Montefeltro, Francis, who climbed on a wall as though he was in a pulpit, began to speak quoting precisely these verses: 'So great is the good that I await that every pain is a delight', words which are in perfect harmony with the audience of the moment, knights met to celebrate the dubbing of a new companion. The story is told on a page of the *Little Flowers*:

> Francis, moved by an inspiration from God, left the valley of Spoleto to go to the Romagna with his companion Brother Leo. And on their way they passed by the foot of the castle and walled village of Montefeltro, where at that time a great banquet and festival were being held to celebrate the knighting of one of the Counts of Montefeltro. When Francis heard from the villagers about the festivity that was taking place, and that many noblemen had gathered there from various districts, he said to Brother Leo, 'Let's go up to that festival, for with God's help we will gather some good spiritual fruit.'
>
> Among the noblemen who had come to that meeting was a great and wealthy count from Tuscany named Orlando of Chiusi in Casentino who, because of the marvellous things he had heard about the holiness and miracles of St Francis, had a great devotion for him and wanted very much to see him and hear him preach.
>
> St Francis arrived at that village and entered and went to the square where all those noblemen were assembled. And in fervour of spirit he climbed on to a low wall and

began to preach, taking as the theme of his sermon these words in the common tongue: 'So great is the good which I expect that all pain is to me a delight.' And under the dictation of the Holy Spirit he preached on this theme so devoutly and so profoundly – proving its truth by the various sufferings and martyrdoms of the holy apostles and martyrs, and by the severe penances of the holy confessors, and by the many tribulations and temptations of the holy virgins and of the other saints – that everyone stood there gazing attentively at him, listening to him as though an angel of God were speaking.

We have recalled almost all the occasions when the future saint spoke in French, at least those of which there are traces in the sources. French is the language of the reading he shared with his former companions, the language of his father's business, the language of his impetuous emotion, indissolubly linked with the springtime dreams of his lay youth. But French is above all the language in which the young Francis once learned the virtues of courage and generosity and forged for himself a moral code, taking as his model the heroic virtues of the knights and paladins; a code and a model which survive, tenaciously, alongside the incomparably profound example that the new convert found in the Gospel, on which from now on he meditated every moment.

There was a novice who longed greatly to possess a psalter. To dissuade him, and to show him the dangers of the culture of books, Francis, at that time gravely ill, told him this story: 'The Emperor Charles, Roland, and Oliver, all paladins and valiant knights who were mighty in battle, pursued the infidels even to death, sparing neither toil nor fatigue, and gained a memorable victory for themselves; and by way of conclusion, these holy martyrs died fighting for the faith of Christ. We see many today who would like to attribute honour and glory to themselves by being content with singing about the exploits of others.' By that he meant that it is not very important to become preoccupied with books or science; virtuous actions count for much more because 'knowledge produces self-importance; love makes the building grow' (here Francis is quoting I Corinthians).

In 1220, a mission to Morocco had ended tragically, with the beheading of five brothers. The episode gave rise to a story which recounted the life and passion of the martyrs. Having learned that his praises and those of the five executed men were being sung everywhere, and seeing that the brothers were boasting of this exploit as if it were their own, Francis rejected the legend, refusing to allow it to be read. He said, ' Let everyone glory in his own martyrdom and not that of others.' This was related by the brave Giordano da Giano, who was sent to Germany against his will in 1221. In 1262 he wrote a perceptive *Chronicle*, full of life, which gives us valuable information about the establishment and development of the Franciscan order on German soil. At the moment when Francis reacted so violently, forbidding the promotion of the cult of the five martyrs, he was around thirty-eight. However, he again reminds us of the words which Chrétien de Troyes attributes to the father of the wicked Meleagant in his *Lancelot*: 'A gentleman need not praise his courage to magnify his act, for the act is its own best praise.' And in *Yvain, The Knight with the Lion*, Kay explains: 'There is a big difference between the braggart and the brave; the braggart tells tall stories about himself around the fire, thinking all his listeners are fools and that no one really knows him. But the brave man would be very upset if he heard his own valiant deeds being told to another.'

In a chapter of *The Mirror of Perfection*, a text from the

beginning of the fourteenth century which brings together the sparse testimony of Francis's companions, the saint dwells at length on the dangers of knowledge and education, which make people proud and lead to forgetfulness of the spirit of love and pure simplicity. The brothers whom Francis prefers and who delight him are those who do not need rich convents, libraries, studies, but who, like the wandering knights of the romances, are ready to put themselves to the test and to meet the challenges that they pose themselves: 'These are my brothers, the knights of the Round Table, who go to uninhabited and remote places to abandon themselves with more love to prayer and meditation, lamenting their own sins and those of others, living in simplicity and humility. Their holiness is known to God and sometimes unknown to the brothers and to other men.'

Francis was always attracted by solitude and needed it; he did not conceive of it in any way as an ascetic flight from the world. He went so far as to codify the practice in a Rule, probably written around 1217–1218, for people who wanted to withdraw periodically into hermitages. The difficulty of reconciling the most rigorous isolation with the material conditions of survival, of uniting the active life of Martha with the contemplative life of Mary (in the Gospel these are the two sisters of Lazarus, whom Jesus raised from the dead) is here resolved in a quite original way: the terms used indicate that Francis wanted the establishment of a particularly fraternal love, and almost family tenderness, among the brothers who had withdrawn into this solitude: 'No more than three or at most four friars should go together to a hermitage to lead a religious life there. Two of these should act as mothers, with the other two, or the other one, as their children. The mothers are to lead the life of Martha; the other two, the life of Mary Magdalene.' During the day, the 'sons' pray and meditate in solitude, under the care of 'mothers' who make their meals and perform all practical tasks, seeing that nothing disturbs the contemplatives. 'Now and then, the sons should exchange places with the others, according to whatever arrangement seems best suited for the moment.' One can envisage these retreats when visiting the hermitage of Le Carceri on the slopes of Monte Subasio, not far from Assisi, or of Greccio in the valley of Rieti, or again of Le Celle near Cortona; these places are hidden in thick woods surrounding by undulating country, broad and gentle.

In 1216 Jacques de Vitry had come to Perugia, there to be consecrated bishop of St John of Acre, on the Palestinian coast. Some days before embarking in Genoa to go to his distant episcopal see, he wrote a letter which reveals a remarkable knowledge of the Franciscan movement. His testimony is doubly important, both because it is so early and because it comes from someone outside the Order. He relates how, when in Perugia, he had witnessed the maltreatment of the corpse of Innocent III, stripped of all its precious vestments and abandoned half-naked in the church in a state of decomposition. Jacques de Vitry had also been present at the election of the dead pontiff's successor, Honorius III. It is not impossible that in Perugia at that time he met Francis, who was certainly present at the death of Innocent III. After painting a terse picture of the intrigues of the Curia ('They were all so occupied with temporal and worldly affairs, questions of kings and kingdoms, disputes and trials, that they hardly ventured to make any statements of a spiritual kind'), he recalls that nevertheless in Umbria he found grounds for hope.

I nonetheless found consolation in seeing a great number of men and women who renounced all their possessions and left the world for the love of Christ: 'Friars Minor' and 'Sisters Minor', as they were called. They are held in great esteem by the Lord Pope and the cardinals. They are totally detached from temporal things and have but one passion to which they devote all their efforts: to snatch from the vanities of the world souls in peril and prevail upon them to imitate their example. During the day [the brothers] go into the cities and villages, giving themselves over to the active life of the apostolate; at night, they return to their hermitage or withdraw into solitude to live the contemplative life. The women live near the cities in various hospices and refuges; they live a community life from the work of their hands, but accept no income. The veneration that the clergy and laity show them is a burden to them.

Here Jacques de Vitry seems to be referring particular to the community of San Damiano, led by Clare; but we shall not be speaking of her and her tormented relationship with Francis until we come to the time of her conversion.

3

'This is What I Wish! This is What I Seek!'

Around three years had passed since the day when Francis had undertaken to follow the orders of the crucifix of San Damiano. Throughout this time he had restored churches and served lepers, but also prayed a great deal, and meditated a great deal on the Gospels, above all that of John, which he knew almost by heart. But that was not enough for the unrest in his great soul.

One Sunday, at mass in the church of the Portiuncula, he heard the passage in which Christ entrusts the apostles with their preaching mission. The future saint had understood this only in a general sense, and Thomas of Celano does not fail to emphasize how, without the irreplaceable mediation of the priest, a lay person's knowledge of the scriptures remained uncertain. So after the mass Francis asked the priest to explain the text to him in detail. This was the decisive illumination: a sudden intuition which in reality was the fruit of a slow and obscure period of underground maturing. 'Francis, hearing that the disciples of Christ should not possess gold or silver or money; nor carry along the way scrip, or wallet, or bread, or a staff; that they should not have shoes, or two tunics; but that they should preach the kingdom of God and penance, immediately cried out exultingly: "This is what I wish, this is what I seek, this is what I long to do with all my heart.'" Bursting with joy, he immediately abandoned his hermit's garb, of which, as we saw, the staff, sandals and leather belt were the distinctive attributes. The Gospel prescribes just one tunic. Francis wanted to go further: he decided that this should be very coarse, of no value, and he replaced the leather belt with a simple knotted cord. He chose a habit with a capuche, a hood, 'that bore a likeness to the cross, so that by means of it he might drive off all temptations of the devil; he designed a very rough tunic, so that by it he might crucify the flesh with all its vices and sins; he designed a very poor and mean tunic, one that would not excite the covetousness of the world.' The learned work of Thomas of Celano, behind its web of biblical quotations, nevertheless allows some typical and very human characteristics of Francis to filter through; these are always stamped with a great humanity. Certainly, like all his contemporaries, he had a certain proneness to 'holy superstition'; thus he felt the need to rely on talismans and thought it possible through certain gestures, rites and objects like the tunic and the cord to enter into communication with the divine. Indeed, Pope Gregory IX stopped himself cursing only by carrying round his neck a relic, the finger of the blessed Marie d'Oignies! There is nothing irreverent in supposing that someone who accepts as an act of faith that a formula pronounced by a man endowed with particular powers can change bread into a divine body will be ready to apply his belief in a super-natural and mysterious life to his own person, his private life, the most modest events.

Take, for example, the case of the cord with three knots, which is so characteristic that it makes it possible to recognize a Franciscan at a glance. The interpretation which sees the three knots as symbolizing the vows of chastity, poverty and obedience is very late: it goes back at most to the sixteenth century. One can see that in the earliest representations of Francis the knots are always there on the cord but that their number varies (from three to seven). The knots probably had the same function as the rough material of the tunic; to quench carnal desires. This explanation is given us by the cleric Henri d'Avranches, in a poem dedicated to the saint which he wrote around 1237. After a kind of self-criticism, an examination of his conscience which ended with a verdict of guilty, Francis 'condemned himself to be girded with a cord with three knots, as if they were real scoundrels, these hips which had borne the fire of an illegitimate passion'. Anthropologically, the knot is the reinforcement of a bond, a pact, a charm: by girding himself with a cord and adding knots, perhaps Francis also wanted to emphasize and recall by an external sign his decision from now on to commit himself to the way of itinerant preaching. The number of knots became fixed at three, because three is a symbolic number: there are three persons of the Trinity, three wise men, and the Gospel has to be opened three times in the *Sortes apostolorum*. Francis had recourse to this rite, which the apostles themselves are said to have practised, at important moments of his life – for example when he was uncertain about what orders to give to Bernard, his first companion, and consequently about the future character of the budding fraternity; or again on La Verna, before the appearance of the seraph, in the hope of knowing the tribulations which would affect the end of his life, which at that time he knew to be very close. In the ceremony of the *Sortes apostolorum*, after prayer one opened the holy book at random; if one came upon the same page three times running, this was certain proof of the will of God: the voice of the Lord was replying directly to the person asking the question. Finally, the cruciform tunic was meant to keep the demons at bay, a concern which never happens to have been an obsession of Francis, though it occupies such a place in the biographies of so many other mediaeval saints.

When he speaks of this famous Sunday at the Portiuncula, Thomas does not cite a particular passage from the Gospels, but a series of verses from Mark, Luke and Matthew all mixed up together. Since the Gospel passage about the mission of the apostles is read on St Luke's Day, 18 October, and St Matthew's Day, 24 February, and the other Franciscan sources all differ on this point, critics have argued for a long time over the precise date (autumn 1208 or winter 1209) on which Francis truly understood what his duty was. Francis himself explicitly declares in the *Testament* that he acted on his own initiative: 'When God gave me some friars, there was no one to tell me what I should do; but the Most High himself made it clear to me that I must live the life of the Gospel.'

Can we suppose that, once again, Francis had recourse to the rite of the *Sortes apostolorum?* The mixture of verses from Matthew, Mark and Luke could be an indication of this: perhaps Thomas of Celano and the other hagiographers did not dare to say it openly, since the use of the *Sortes apostolorum*, while tolerated, was not truly orthodox, and to base the origins of the Order of the Friars Minor on a superstitious gesture could seem a false note. In the episode concerning Bernard, is not care taken to explain that, if Francis opened the book three times, it was by virtue of his love for the Trinity?

It is again a garment which is the agent and sign of the new change, which this time was much more decisive than the transition from a lay garment to that of a hermit. On close inspection, Francis's choice was a refusal to choose. He meant to be dressed as a poor man, in what came to hand, without any 'uniform' or attribute to indicate that he belonged to a category which could benefit from the least appreciation, as was precisely the case with the hermit. He did not even choose a particular colour, which could have been a manifest symbol of his vocation. From the beginning, the future saint, and later the first companions, wore material of a faded colour, from grey and dark brown to pale green, simply because these were less expensive, whereas fabrics of bright colours were particularly expensive. That is why in one of the scenes in the series from the Franciscan church of Pistoia, painted in the middle of the thirteenth century and still preserved in the local museum, the Franciscans, gathered around the body of their dead founder, are all represented in robes of different colours, but always within the range of pale colours. Francis never bothered to select a common colour which would immediately indicate the Order to which those who were in it belonged, whereas among the Capuchins (the last branch to be born of the Franciscan stem), the colour of the robe became so typical and constant that for all of us it is synonymous with foaming milk and coffee – cappuccino.

Right down to the matter of dress, the saint proclaimed that he was going to approach poverty in a different way. It was not that the church did not help the needy and distressed in his time. But it had never put itself in question as a privileged structure: it had never departed from its certainties or its established positions. By the conditions in which they lived, their culture, the guarantee of a solid well-being, the clergy maintained between themselves and the host of the disinherited a clear frontier which could not be crossed. To assess the first of the extraordinary innovations made by Francis, which nevertheless all derive from a simple concern to follow the gospel to the letter, we should recall that it was strictly forbidden for monks and clergy to beg: and by clergy were understood all those who had at least received the tonsure, or had joined one of the sacred orders which preceded the priesthood. The ban was again repeated by the Council of Paris in 1213–1214; the superiors had to provide a horse and sustenance for religious who travelled: to ask for alms was to put oneself in an embarrassing position, in danger, even sin. The *Three Companions* do not fail to emphasize the novelty vigorously: 'At this time no one dared to give up their riches and their possessions and ask for charity from door to door.'

Although Francis made religious commitment his *raison d'être*, he never thought of becoming a priest or monk. He decided not to cross the limits within which the laity lived; it was within this space that he chose to act. It was not by chance that he compared his brothers to a little *flock* sent by God, and not to the *shepherds* of this flock. Resolved to remain in a situation of weakness and subjection, he wanted to steep himself, with no distinguishing mark, in this society which the church could guide in many ways: and he chose to belong to its poorest, most scorned part, to which the humble workers on the land also belonged.

As the gospel prescribes, he did not judge. By avoiding any criticism or condemnation of the corrupt morals of the church, by refusing to take part in reform projects, to make the least claim for a more active role of the faithful, Francis escaped the great danger of joining the ranks of those who saw themselves irresistibly driven to rebellion and guilty dissidence. On the contrary, in time the Friars Minor were regarded as a basic aid in taming and bringing within orthodoxy all the ferment and the desire for more intense participation in the religious life, characteristics of a society engaged in a marked change, but which the church on the defensive had rejected as heretical instead of trying to absorb them. Moreover Francis's profound respect for Rome and his loyalty to it excluded any danger of deviance.

Francis professed a respectful and prudent detachment from an ecclesiastical organization which had not ceased to grow throughout history. He nevertheless affirmed with an always passionate and sincere emphasis his obedience to the priests, even to those who proved unworthy and whose moral conduct was deplorable. He was driven by a vital need to enter physically into contact with Christ, to touch the divine body through the eucharist, and for this sacrament the mediation of the priest was indispensable for him, as it was for all the laity. Right up to his deathbed Francis obstinately refused to ask privileges from the Curia and indicated to his brothers that they should not do so either. He respected the church, but it was in the footsteps of Christ that he followed, and Christ's words which he applied. Thus one day, when he had been invited to a meal by Cardinal Ugolino, the future Pope Gregory IX, he did not hesitate to ask beforehand the alms of a few pieces of bread. He then put them on the richly adorned table, thus embarrassing the prelate and the other guests. After the meal his host reprimanded him in private, with affection and indulgence, addressing him as 'my very simple brother'. Francis defended himself against having offended Ugolino's dignity: 'Indeed I have done a great honour, by honouring a greater Lord, because God is pleased with poverty and above all with voluntary begging. For my part I think it royal dignity and nobility to follow the Lord who though rich made himself poor among us.' Francis's reply is that of the obsequious vassal: if a subject performs the obedience due to his lord, at the same time he is honouring the lord and his representative; but he puts an immeasurable distance between his interlocutor and himself.

With a tranquil assurance, in fact Francis is making a leap

backward in time; he meets up with the apostles, whose life he shares, when they were still on their way by the Master's side without any structure or organization. A passage of his *Admonitions* is very revealing in this respect: the brothers 'honour clergy who live according to the laws of the holy Roman Church', but themselves observe 'the gospel of our Lord Jesus Christ, living in obedience, in chastity and with no possessions'. (The term clergy is generic, but it is evident that Francis was thinking here of priests who were responsible for the spiritual government of the faithful and the celebration of the sacraments.) He himself, however, intended to live out his religious commitment in a different way, not only from priests but also from another kind of religious who had not necessarily received the priesthood: the monks.

To become a monk one had to make a double promise: to change the customs of one's previous life and never to leave the monastery one had entered. For the monk, the horizon therefore shrank to the narrow limits of the monastery, the rule of which excluded the faithful. For the priest, the edifice of the church certainly opened up to welcome the laity, but these had to be impelled there by their devotion. For Francis, the place of the religious life is an open space to be crossed on a perpetual journey. The difference in his attitude appears, among other things, in a detail which might make one smile but which is neverthe-less revealing. In his Rule, St Benedict had stipulated that monks should wear breeches only on journeys, for reasons of modesty and convenience, since they might need to raise their habits to protect them from the mud or to have more freedom in their movements; on their return to the monastery these garments, duly washed, had to be given back to the superior. Francis, who wanted a minimum habit for his brothers, one that was reduced to essentials, nevertheless made the breeches a permanent piece of clothing, since he and his companions could never conceive themselves as being other than on a journey.

He did not wait for people to come to meet him; he went out to seek them. Indefatigably throughout his life, he went through villages and cities, taking any way which led to men and women. He spoke to them by the roadside and in the fields, where he shook hands with the peasants; he preached in the open air, in squares whether the heart of urban life was beating, and went into houses, into the bosoms of families, inaugurating a greeting which aroused amazement, even stupor, although it was prescribed by Christ to the apostles: 'The Lord give you peace!'

Peace. When Francis was around twenty-two, the Crusaders of the Fourth Crusade (1203–1204) conquered Constantinople. Four years later the church unleashed the so called 'Albigensian' Crusade against the Cathar heresy: it was to last until 1229 and was accompanied by horrible massacres and destruction in the cities of Albi, Toulouse and Carcassonne. The Cathars conceived of the world as a battlefield in which good and evil were in confrontation: God, creator of the spirit, against Satan, creator of matter. They preached moral renewal and a heightened asceticism, and condemned marriage, procreation, private property, the exercise of justice and war. But it was precisely because of this moral rigour that the movement had become a formidable adversary of the Catholic Church, whose members, by contrast, were marked by lax customs and mediocre religious preparation. In 1212 the Spanish Christians engaged in a bloody battle against the Muslim Arabs at Las Navas de Tolos in Andalucia. There was war everywhere: between the papacy and the empire; between one city and another; within the same city; between the different factions. Assisi did not escape the rule.

In 1210, one of the many fragile peace treaties had been signed there; however, this differed from the others since it also marked the real birth of the commune. According to this treaty, the *maiores*, the greater, gave up their domination of the *minores* who had previously been personally dependent on them. This is the first time that the two terms appear in documents from Assisi. The citizens were no longer 'someone's men', but the men of the commune, and the obligations of one man to another disappeared in favour of a dependence of the individual on the community. Certainly peace did not suppress the development of a marked hierarchy within civil society, as is shown by the very terms used in the treaty (which excluded all the countryfolk). But who were the *maiores* and the *minores* in Assisi? If we look at similar documents, the statutes of other communes, for example those of Anghiari from the end of the thirteenth century, we can see that the *maiores* correspond to the judges and the knights, capable of getting themselves horses and armour for war; the *minores* are the humble cultivators tilling the earth. To simplify things somewhat, in Assisi we may see the *maiores* as the *boni homines* of the old days, nobles and the powerful, and the *minores* as all the other citizens except the countryfolk. Of course it is easy to regard the choice made by Francis, who defines himself and his brothers as *minores*, as an echo of the struggles which set two social categories against each other: those who live in wretched subjection and those who, by contrast, exercise power and a harsh authority. Be this as it may, *minor* is above all a term taken from the Gospel: when the apostles began to discuss in hierarchical terms which among them was the greatest (*maior*), Christ called them, put a child in their midst, and told them, cradling it in his arms: 'Whoever receives this little child in my name receives me, and whoever receives me receives him who sent me; for he among you who is the least (*minor*) shall be the greatest (*maior*).' Mark adds: 'Whoever among you wishes to be the first, he shall become the last of all and the servant of all.' Both meanings, the political and the religious, intertwine in Francis's decision when in the sixth chapter of the *Regula non bullata* he prescribes: 'No one is to be called "Prior". They are all to be known as "Friars Minor" without distinction, and they should be prepared to wash one another's feet.' Being 'less' expresses a concept to which Francis always remained faithful and which he defended ceaselessly all his life: to continue to share the precarious life of the outcast, the poor and the weak, which in his view was the only means of escaping the logic of a power which condemned people to defend the good that they had acquired and to see anyone who coveted it as an enemy. Francis replied to Bishop Guido of Assisi, who advised him in a fatherly way to relax the excessively rigid behaviour of the brotherhood ('I find the kind of life that you have adopted, namely desiring to possess nothing and to have nothing in this world, harsh and rough), in these terms: 'Lord, if we had goods, we would also have to have arms to defend them. It is from wealth that questions and lawsuits come, and thus the love of God and the love of neighbour are hindered in many ways. Therefore we do not want to have any possessions in this world.' Francis stops there: he does not add the easy corollary, 'And you too must change.' This is another point to emphasize; in the saint's project one can only lead others to change and correct themselves by example. It is the example that must convince, even more than words: and again these words must never have the tone of an attack or an accusation, but must be a simple brotherly exhortation on equal terms.

When Christ, in a passage which so struck Francis at the Portiuncula, prescribes to the apostles that they should go through the world without gold or money, with bare feet and just one tunic, he adds that they must not be afraid of being deprived of everything, 'for the labourer is worthy of his hire' (Matt.10.10). Thus the apostles' spirit of poverty and detachment did not dispense those who received spiritual benefits from providing for their sustenance. In his generous extremism, Francis did not choose the life of the apostles as a model: he looked directly to Christ, who was eternally poor and a pilgrim. Here again he was not content with what he read. He went beyond precepts, since to accept support from the community was to open the door to situations of privilege; it was in a way to choose to lie among the pastors and no longer among the sheep; and that would have been to refuse to share to the end the life of the poor, deprived of everything, even rights. Aware of what was at stake, Thomas of Celano and the *Three Companions* avoid quoting the verse 'the labourer is worthy of his hire' which follows the words of Christ forbidding the possession of gold, silver and sandals, saying that one must be content with one tunic. In his project Francis was inspired, rather, by Psalm 127.2, 'You will profit from the labour of your hands, blessed shall you be', and from Paul's Second Letter to the Thessalonians, 3.10: 'If anyone will not work, let him not eat.'

In the *Testament*, he again energetically reaffirms the obligation for brothers to engage in manual work: at the point of death he recalls how, in the first days after his conversion, he worked in the leper colonies and, certainly astonishing those who listened to him, repeated his firm intention of continuing to work: 'I worked with my own hands and I am still determined to work.'

Francis and the first brothers worked almost anywhere they could make themselves useful: in the fields, in the olive harvest, in the forest transporting wood, in the cities dis-

tributing water and building walls; in the houses serving
with humility; in the leper colonies looking after the sick
poor whom no one would approach. Anyone who before
joining the brotherhood had not only strength to work –
two hands and two arms – but had also practised a craft
could and was even required to keep the instruments of his
craft and apply himself to what he knew how to do, provided that this was a licit and honest trade: thus, while he
was forbidden to continue to exercise the work of a
merchant or a butcher, we know of brothers who were
tailors, smiths or potters. Francis refused to teach illiterate
brothers to read, but he required those who did not know
how to work with their hands to acquire technical skills. He
himself had become skilful in making baskets and pots. One
day even, absorbed in his task, he forgot to pray attentively;
ashamed, he threw the basket on the fire, saying to the
brothers: 'It is vanity to allow oneself to be distracted by
imagination and useless follies when at the time of prayer
we are speaking to the great King.'

Francis's hostility to knowledge and culture did not
stem from a reactionary attitude, but this position nevertheless ran counter to the atmosphere of the time: at that
moment the church needed increasing education of those
who fought in its ranks to combat heresy. Nor did it hesitate to support the Dominicans' choice of the 'book', since
the Dominicans identified as their main task the trans-
mission of a well-founded refutation of heresy, principally
to the Cathars, who they wanted to suffer an inescapable
defeat.

However, the possession of books, which were valuable
luxury items, could only be contrary to Francis's ideal of
complete renunciation and absolute poverty. Moreover he
doubted knowledge as being a source of pride and domination, of division between the brothers, stifling affection and

reciprocal charity among them. After his conversion he had not gone out in search of companions or disciples, whose leader he could have become. For any Christian worthy of the name it was enough to hear the words of the gospel and follow in the footsteps of Christ, brother of man because he is Son of God. He was the only point of reference needed. When by chance Francis, in a spirit of charity, exhorted and admonished those who had gone astray, he did so as one equal to another. He did not plan to found an Order: the word completely absent from his vocabulary.

The companions were a gift from the Most High. And since they were companions and not converted disciples, at least until he was forced by his extraordinary success to provide one, Francis did not foresee any structure within the community. Another of his great innovations was to have given birth to a brotherhood essentially composed of lay people, without the creation of the slightest difference of consideration or treatment within it when priests and scholars, who had attended the universities, joined it; and it was like this in the first period.

The church, initially mistrustful, soon understood the considerable role that the Franciscans could play in containing and extinguishing the heretical movements and their polemic. Thanks to the brothers, it could show that in its midst there was a positive model for the laity, a pole capable of attracting and channelling all the ferments of the new times, all the movements in the face of which its own structures had proved to be rigid or inadequate. After Francis's death, the force of tradition inevitably took the upper hand, with a marked clericalization of the order. By the bull *Ordinem Vestrum* dated 14 November 1245, Innocent IV prohibited the order from accepting illiterate candidates, in other words those who did not know Latin, and even encouraged the recruitment of the Friars Minor in university centres. Happily Francis did not see any of this, but he foresaw it.

He tried to show the novice who asked to be allowed to have a psalter the slope on to which this dangerous desire would lure him. This is what the *Legend of Perugia* tells us. As Francis was seated in front of the fire to warm himself, the novice returned to the charge with the question of the psalter. The saint replied to him: 'And when you have a psalter, you will want a breviary, and when you have a breviary, you will install yourself in a chair like a great prelate, and you will order your brother: "Bring me my breviary!"' Francis's discourse ended with an unexpected, somewhat theatrical, gesture, but one which cannot have failed to have a great psychological effect. 'As he said this he was carried away with deep emotion, took some ashes from the hearth, sprinkled them on his head and rubbed some on himself, repeating: "That's the breviary!" The brother was completely dumbfounded and ashamed.' The ashes evidently evoked the condition of human beings, heirs of Adam and his fault, whose sin condemns them to become ashes again. The true Christian must meditate on his condition with a sincere heart; he must recollect himself rather than find pleasure and distraction in the sacred books or, worse, take pleasure in them and be proud of being able to understand the arcane details of the scriptures. Francis's true library is his memory: he required his followers to learn his letters, the *Admonitions* and the Rule by heart. In this way he could remove the disparity between the illiterate and the learned; but he also wanted memory, applied to a few texts constantly repeated, to reinforce reflection and concentration.

The story of the novice is not quite over. Francis, not wanting to leave this young man mortified, immediately told him his own experience, to give him both an example and a concrete application. He began with a personal confession: 'I too, Brother, was tempted to have books; but that I might know God's will on this point I took the book of the Gospels and I asked the Lord to make it known to me on the first page where I opened the book what he wanted of me.' The rite, with which we are now familar, produced the verse: 'The secret of the kingdom of God is given to you, but to those who are outside everything comes with parables.' It was as if to say that it is better to address oneself directly to God through prayer and personal reflection than through the tortuous intermediary of yesterday's words. Francis's renunciation was sincere; however, the abandonment of the pleasure of reading must have been all the more painful, since in his youth he had read romances and poems.

Among Francis' writings, the very fine page that he dictates to Brother Leo, probably in the evening of his life, is particularly revealing. It seeks to explain what for him, and therefore for his companions, must be the perfect and true joy. Perfect joy is not to learn that bishops and archbishops, masters of theology in Paris, kings of France and England, have entered the order; it is not even to know that all the infidels have been converted, or to discover that one can perform miracles. For Francis, perfect joy is to arrive after a long journey at the Portiuncula, in the middle of the night, weary, wet and muddy and with icicles on the edge of one's tunic which keep striking one's legs so that they bleed. And after knocking to be driven away by the one who opens the door with these words: 'Go away. You are a simple and uneducated fellow. From now on don't stay with us any more. We are so many and so important that we don't need you.' To bear these words with patience, and not to be upset is true joy; here Christ, betrayed by his own, persecuted and insulted at the beginning of the passion, is the evident model. The *Little Flowers*, which contain a story very close to this, add some other conditional statements, other key motifs of perfect joy: 'Brother Leo, even if a Friar Minor knew all languages and all sciences and Scripture . . . the courses of the stars and the powers of herbs . . . the qualities of birds and fishes, animals, humans, roots, trees, rocks, and waters . . .' Francis is thinking here of the wisdom of King Solomon as it is described in the Bible, and does not want to rival it, even in a dream. He does not aspire to culture, but to humble manual work.

In exchange for their labour, the brothers can receive food which allows them to live: that is the meaning that Francis attaches to the word 'alms'. But there is no question of providing for the next day; it was even forbidden to put the next day's vegetables to soak in the evening, since trust in providence had to be unlimited, the situation one of absolute precariousness. Above all, the brothers were never to receive money on any pretext, not even in conditions of the most extreme need: the only exception allowed, which was to be resorted to as rarely as possible, was to feed and help the lepers. To accept offerings of money, said Francis, is to steal from the poor. That should be enough to show us the transformation that his Order had to undergo in time, to the point of becoming synonymous with the 'mendicant' Order. ('Alms is the legacy and the due right owed to the poor; it has been gained for us by Our Lord Jesus Christ. And the brothers who work to gain it will have great reward . . .') . This respect for the rights of the poor is recalled in Chapter IX of the *Regula non bullata*. It is again recalled in Chapter VI of the *Regula bullata*, where, however, Francis has to drop the allusion to work.

Here some explanation needs to be given of the Rules. The text of the First Rule, which Innocent III approved orally, has been lost. What we call the First Rule is in reality the Second Rule: it was proposed to the General Chapter which met in 1221, but needed so many exceptions and reservations on the part of both the brothers and the Roman Curia that it remained *non bullata*, i.e. it did not obtain the approval of the pontifical seal. After a series of fruitless efforts and grave compromises, a new Rule was approved in 1223 which was then called *bullata*. However, it no longer respected the saint's original programme.

Francis himself never yielded. He became even more rigorous about himself, since he judged it his duty to offer a living example of faithfulness to the plan of life which he had once required his companions to share. The *Legend of Perugia* mentions that he often repeated to the brothers: 'I have never been a robber. I mean of alms which are the heritage of the poor, taking always less than I needed so as not to defraud the poor. To do otherwise would be robbery.'

He always had almost a horror of money, even money earned. As a former merchant he was aware of the ravages wrought by possessing it, which stifle any desire of charity in favour of greed and cupidity. He did not hesitate to punish the companions for any infringement of this rule, however light: he was a man of violent passions which sometimes drove him into a fury. One day a devotee entered the little church of the Portiuncula and left money by the crucifix. A brother who was passing picked it up and immediately put it on the window sill. Francis reproved him harshly, and forced him to take the money and keep it in his mouth until he had put it on a donkey's droppings.

He used to say that money is simply dirt to be crushed underfoot; that it must be treated like excrement and be shunned like the devil in person. One day he found himself at Bari with a companion: the two were travelling along a road when they saw a purse full of money on the road. The companion immediately wanted to pick it up and give the contents to the poor. Francis refused, saying that this was a ruse of the devil. His companion was not convinced. A little later he retraced his steps, and instead of the money he found a snake. One cannot swear to the truth of this episode, which Thomas of Celano reports only in his *Second Life*, written about twenty years after the saint's death. The model of the story is biblical: in Genesis the devil as tempter appears in the form of a serpent. At all events, if we are to understand Francis's obsession with money, the fact that he associates it so clearly with the divine curse which struck the first couple at the moment of the Fall is very revealing. However, at first sight it might seem amazing that the saint never emphasizes Judas's greed. For Francis, the desperate Judas, who took his life by hanging himself, is not the 'very bad merchant' (*mercator pessimus*) as depicted by so many representations of hell at the end of the twelfth century, because he sold his Master for thirty pieces of silver. The ideology of chivalry is so powerful in Francis that it leads him to emphasize the enormity of the treason with sadness. In Chapter XXII of the *Regula non bullata* he admonishes his companions in these terms: 'Remember the words of our Lord, "Love your enemies, do good to those who hate you." Our Lord Jesus Christ himself, in whose footsteps we must follow, called the man who betrayed him his friend, and gave himself up of his own accord to his executioners.' Judas is the vassal who betrays his Lord and denies him, the one who tramples on the supreme virtues, loyalty and faithfulness.

If Francis sometimes allowed himself to be overcome with anger, the dominant note in his community was neither rigour, nor punishment, nor harsh penances, which in any case were expressly forbidden: on the contrary, it was joy. The Gospel of St Matthew had revealed to him these words of Christ: 'When you fast, do not put on a sombre air like the hypocrites; they have a sad face so that one can see that they fast. Truly, I say to you, they already have their reward' (6.16–17). One looks in vain for such a recommendation in the monastic rules, whereas for Francis it becomes a precept of life, introduced from the *Regula non bullata* onwards: thus in Chapter VII he orders: 'They should let it be seen that they are happy in God, cheerful and courteous, as is expected of them, and be careful not to appear gloomy or depressed like hypocrites.'

This precept, which forbids hypocritical sadness, was then suppressed in the *Regula bullata*. However, it expresses all the importance that Francis attaches to perfect accord between the inner person and the outer person: thus the demons whose thoughts Francis manages to imagine find themselves reduced to impotence: 'Since this servant of God preserves his joy in tribulation as well as in prosperity, we can find no way to harm his soul.' This passage on spiritual joy taken from the *Legend of Perugia* shows us at third hand the voice of Francis when he rebuked a sad companion and when, conversely, he said that he was strengthened by a smiling face. He apostrophizes the companion in these terms: 'Why do you display the sadness and sorrow that you feel for your sins that way? It is a matter between you and God. Pray to him that in his goodness he give you the joy of salvation. In my presence and in the presence of others, try to be always joyful, for it is not fitting that a servant of God appear before the brothers or other men with a sad and glum face.'

He himself admits readily: 'Conversely, if I happen to be tempted and downcast, I need only contemplate the joy of a companion and I go from the temptation and despondency to interior joy.'

Thus it is that Francis loved poverty, inseparable from

joy. In fact his poverty is a voluntary and liberating poverty, which provides spiritual immunity from the thirst for domination and possessions, from violence, desires elevated to needs, the constraints of everyday life. Voluntary poverty is physical freedom, which forces one to go on endlessly, but above all it is freedom of spirit, since it allows people truly to listen to the words of the gospel and to love without reserve.

Whereas the monks, shut up in their monasteries which they cannot leave, lament their sins supported by the wealth of the community, and priests and canons still have common interests to defend, Francis and his companions live like the true poor, in a space open to the world, united by the brotherly love of a harmonious family. Often Francis thought of himself as a woman, in particular a mother, thus expressing in his own way the tenderness and love of Christ, but also feminine humility and submission, translated and put to work in the concrete setting of domestic relationships.

In his *Chronicle*, Thomas of Eccleston relates the first arrival of the brothers in England, in 1224: in Canterbury they had found lodging in a small room under a building which housed a school of priests. At nightfall, when the students returned home, the brothers entered the deserted school; they lit a fire and sat round it. They would talk and meditate while drinking, in tranquil simplicity, beer diluted with hot water. However, in Salisbury 'they drank round the fire at the time of conversation with such good humour and joy that he was thought happy who could take the cup from his neighbour in jest in order to drink.' Like children and young people who laugh every time they meet – and this is perhaps the great difference between them and adults – the brothers, above all the younger ones, burst out laughing at their first ecnounter. However, since they certainly laughed too often, at table as well, an extreme remedy was adopted: any burst of laughter was punished with a beating. In spite of that, one poor brother was beaten eleven times in one day; yet even this did not make him stop laughing. He stopped only when the father guardian terrified him into doing his duty by telling him of a terrible dream.

Thomas of Eccleston also recalls that at that time there was no limitation of any kind on the quality of food and wine. For example, Brother Peter of Tewkesbury, minister of the province of Germania, ordered a melancholy brother as a penance to drink a good cup of excellent wine. He then said to him: 'Dearest brother, if you did this penance more often you would also have a better conscience.' To accept everything that is offered in a spirit of love is a prescription which Francis had read in the Gospel of Luke (10.8): however, he is original in having introduced this precept into the *Regula non bullata*: 'In obedience to the Gospel, they may eat any food put before them.' This feature, preserved in the *Regula bullata*, indicates Francis's originality: in fact it was contrary to all the monastic directives, which rigorously regulated the quality and quantity of food, making this norm a fundamental point of asceticism and penitence. Francis's precept was so innovative that it provoked a series of rebellions in the community when the founder, driven by his missionary zeal, left Italy to go to the East. But we shall be considering that later.

Whereas throughout his life Francis mortified his fragile and sick body with penances which he himself subsequently thought excessive, because he regarded himself as a living example for the community and for everyone (he often called his body 'brother ass', to be maltreated without over-much concern), he was always very understanding towards his companions and his neighbours. One night a young brother who had joined the group recently began to cry that he was dying of hunger; during the previous days he had in fact fasted with excessive rigour. The brothers woke up, someone lit a lamp and Francis immediately began to lay the table. They all began to eat in the middle of the night because the saint did not want the young man to feel humiliated eating all alone. The meal was followed by a short sermon on the need to take account of the demands and complexion of one's own body: 'Just as we must try not to eat too much, which harms the body and the soul, so, even more, we must avoid excessive abstinence, since the Lord prefers mercy to sacrifice' (again a quotation from Matt.12.7).

With a smiling and affectionate understanding of human psychology Francis succeeded in converting thieves who sometimes came to ask for a little bread, 'driven by an imperious necessity'. This detail was enough for him: these were not detestable brigands, but poor men. The scene is the hermitage above Borgo San Sepolcro, surrounded by dense woods. First of all Francis advised the brothers to take food to the wood in which the band was hidden and to call out, 'Brother robbers, come! We are the brothers and we are bringing good bread and good wine'; then, he urged them to introduce eggs and cheese gradually into subsequent meals in addition to bread and wine. Only when the meal was over could the brothers allow themselves to give some edifying advice. The episode ends with the robbers, touched by the friendship and amiability shown to them by the brothers, offering to make themselves useful by transporting wood to the hermitage; some even went so far as to make themselves brothers, and others promised from thenceforth to live by the works of their hands.

Sometimes, by one of those sheer contradictions which make him such a sympathetic figure, Francis decided also to ask something for himself. This happened in Rieti, where he had an illness of the eyes. He sent for a brother who used to play the lute when he was in the world and asked him secretly to borrow an instrument. 'Bring it here so that with it you may give some wholesome comfort to brother body that is so full of pains.' However, his companion refused to satisfy this desire: 'I am not a little ashamed to do so, Father, because I am afraid men may suspect that I am being tempted to frivolity.' And the invalid, rather than becoming an object of scandal, kept silent and did not press him further. However, the next night he heard the most marvellous sound of a lute, which seemed to be going back and forth, and this brought the invalid much joy. The next day Francis summoned the brother, told him what had happened, and ended with satisfaction, in a way which was not very saintly but very human: 'The Lord who consoles the afflicted has never left me without consolation. For behold, I who could not hear the lutes of men have heard a far sweeter lute.' The hesitant brother was probably Brother Pacificus. Before he was converted he was called 'the king of verses' because he was the most famous of profane singers and himself the author of worldly songs. In short, the glory of the world had made him so famous that he was crowned in most magnificent fashion by the emperor [Frederick II]; Thomas of Celano records this in his *Second Life* of the saint. Pacificus had been thunderstruck by Francis's preaching; doubtless he was surprised, then fascinated, to discover in the one addressing edifying words to him the same passion that he had for singing, music and profane reading. It is no coincidence that the recollection of a romance finds its way into a religious context and gives the form of a vision to the feelings of admiration which Pacificus had for the one who had 'made him at peace with the Lord'. This is the story. Pacificus, praying before the crucifix, was waiting for Francis in a deserted church – this was the church of St Peter at Bovara, which had been deserted since Trevi, the neighbouring city, had been razed to the ground in 1213. The brother saw 'among many thrones in heaven one which was more beautiful than the others, adorned with precious stones and quite radiant'; a divine inspiration revealed to him that 'this throne had belonged to a fallen angel, and was now reserved for the humble Francis'. The thrones of the heavenly court, empty after the fall of Lucifer (Isa.14.12) and the rebellious angels, are here superimposed on the empty throne in expectation of the coming of the divine judge in Psalm 9.8–9; this is a theme that Pacificus could have admired, for example, in the mosaic in Santa Maria Maggiore in Rome. But here there is also the recollection of the 'throne perilous' on which no one may sit since it is reserved for Galahad, 'the perfect one', in the romance of *The Quest of the Holy Grail.*

Much time had elapsed between this vision and Francis's illness. And it could have been that Pacificus's devotion had been remarkably weakened, since he had come to attach more importance to the judgment of other people than to the desire of the sick Francis. At the end of his life, when his condition became even worse, from time to time Francis dared to ask for a little treat: crayfish, which he loved to eat, pike, aromatic herbs. Sometimes providence intervened by granting him surprise visits from people with baskets and well-filled plates; at other times it took a miracle out of all proportion to the modesty of the request: for example, for a brother who had not wanted to go in search of it neverthe-less to find a small bunch of parsley. From now on Francis needed to be looked after continuously; the brothers found the task of nursing him very painful: the joy and brotherly affection of the first days had disappeared. It was no longer the venerated and undisputed founder who was lying on his bed but an exhausted man, a saint whose death was awaited impatiently so that his tormented body could become a very precious and miraculous relic. But at the point of the story we have now reached, that is a long way off; Francis, a happy man, was enjoying the blossoming of his friendship with Bernard, his first companion.

4

The Companions, The First Rules, Clare

Just as the Pharisee Nicodemus came by night in order to be able to talk quietly with Christ and to receive his teaching in private, and then became a great supporter (John 3.1–21), so one evening 'a holy man' of Assisi, called Bernard, welcomed Francis in his house as his teacher. They spent much of the night in serious and profound discussion. Won over by Francis's example, Bernard, who was very rich, had in fact decided to share his ideals completely, adopting the same clothing and the same life. In the morning they went together to the church of St Nicolas, where they proceeded to perform the rite of the *Sortes apostolorum* in company with another man, by the name of Peter, who had joined them in the meantime. The book of the Gospels was opened three times at passages in Matthew and Luke which prescribed precisely what they wanted to hear: they had to sell everything, distribute the proceeds to the poor, deny themselves and be ready to follow Christ at the risk of their lives.

With great joy, they found that they were brothers: 'From then on they lived according to the precept of the holy Gospel as the Lord had shown them.' Shortly afterwards, the priest Sylvester joined the new family. He was an important recruit because he was an official member of the church who was preferring the company of laymen; his

official position in the ecclesiastical hierarchy was to allow
him one day to be the authorized guarantor of Francis's
sanctity. The future saint had bought stones from him to
rebuild San Damiano. At this time Sylvester was still
greedy, and when he saw Bernard lavishing so much wealth
– for this is how he saw the shower of money distributed to
the poor – he was seized by envy and greed. He asked for
more money for the stones that he was selling. Francis then
put his hand into his friend's pocket and gave the greedy
man several fistfuls of money. This gesture fired the priest,
who brooded on the episode for days: 'Am I not a miserable
man, old as I am, to be avid for temporal goods, when this
young man despises and hates them for the love of God?'
He had a dream which decided him: 'He saw an immense
cross reaching to the sky, and its foot was planted in the
mouth of Francis, while the arms spread from one end of
the world to the other. On awaking, the priest realized and
was convinced that blessed Francis was indeed the friend
and servant of Jesus Christ and that the form of religion he
was introducing would spread over the entire earth.' He
began by leading the life of a penitent in his own home;
then he came down to the plain, reached the cabin near the
Portiuncula which Francis and three companions occupied,
and was with them all his life.

The rampart of mistrust which surrounded the little
community gradually crumbled, but it had not yet fallen
completely. Won over by his enthusiasm, fascinated by the
power of his words, other companions soon joined Francis.
These were extraordinary men who were not afraid either
to break with their own habits or to renounce all material or
emotional security in order to share the life of an improvised
community, with no prestige or tradition; people in very
great moral tension, with abundant virtues, whose religious
commitment was absolute. And then there was the crowd

which listened, sometimes lukewarm; sometimes disconcerted, not to say hostile; sometimes persuaded and won over. There were those who thought that these men who were always ready to exhort others to conversion, to love God, to make peace, were madmen or maniacs; and there were those who, on the contrary, admired them as men leading the life of the gospel. One day someone in the audience was heard to remark: 'Either these men are following the Lord in great perfection, or they must be demented, since their way of life appears desperate, with little food and going about barefoot and clad in the poorest garments.' Young girls took flight, terrified, simply on seeing them in the distance: were not these wild men of the woods, real savages? They were taken as charlatans, possible thieves, and refused hospitality. Francis and his companions often had to take refuge in a church porch or a baking oven. Some greeted them with fistfuls of mud, and others mocked them and forced them to hold dice in their hands; or again, they were seized by their hoods and dragged like sacks carried on the shoulders. The reactions were particularly violent and hostility flared up especially where they had broken family ties and the separation was still bitterly resented.

However, faithful to the words of the gospel, Francis and the companions did not respond to the persecutions and behaved peacefully. This way of life, both austere and cheerful, was disconcerting and troubling, yet ultimately proved attractive. If they were asked, they simply said that they were penitents from Assisi. Francis's call is a fascinating one, calling for peace and love of neighbour. Often the companions formed a chorus, approving what he said and saying that his advice was excellent. Sometimes Francis sang the praises of the Lord, again in French, in a high clear voice, to keep up his courage and that of his companions.

This was a period of apprenticeship and trial and error. Francis experimented with numerous 'rules', none of which has come down to us, different ways of life which he tested in practice with his companions before making them normative principles. He passionately exalted poverty.

On the tympanum of the main porch of the church of Mary Magdalene in Vézélay (1120–1132) there is a gigantic Christ, sending rays of fire (which signify the descent of the Holy Spirit) down on the apostles, thus giving them the ability to preach and to convert. In the lunette and the architrave there are depictions of all the peoples on earth, including those whom a fabulous geography depicts as monstrous races, made inaccessible by the circle of the ocean. The sculptor has resolved at a stroke the problem of impossible salvation (this was to torment so many theologians after the discovery of America: how could the people whom no disciple of Christ had ever reached avoid eternal damnation?). At Vézélay the message is reassuring: the whole of the inhabited earth is moving in time towards the encounter with the Redeemer: this encounter is made historically possible by his sacrifice and the spread of his word through the disciples. The Christ represented on the great maps of mediaeval geography has the same significance: we see him there embracing the disc of the earth, which allows only the divine face, hands and feet to appear.

Francis did not know Vézélay or any of these figured maps of the world; however, one would like to think that he would have enjoyed looking at them and discovering a presentation of his plan: to pursue resolutely, with companions, the mission of the apostles which seemed to have been interrupted. Thomas of Celano feels the painful contrast between the first Franciscan brotherhood, composed of resolute men with a fervent enthusiasm and ready for any sacrifice, and the multitude of brothers of his time, forgetful of this heroic past. And to exalt not only Francis but all the little community, he attributes to the community a supernatural vision in the saint's absence. One night a fiery chariot, on which was a luminous globe like the sun, entered the cabin where the brothers were sleeping and praying. The intense brightness not only enabled them to see material objects, but also made the thoughts of each brother transparent to the others: this was a kind of domestic Pentecost.

Sometimes, however, the brothers took fright at this grandiose project, which entailed having no fear of torture, or injustice, or adversity, and travelling to distant countries in the midst of unknown people. They would have liked to be fervent disciples, but they did not succeed in following Francis's bold imagination which unfolded endlessly, always a little beyond the common horizon. To save the whole of humanity, without exception, Christ wanted the apostles and their successors to bear his word over all the earth. Francis wanted no less. When Sylvester sees the immense cross reaching from the saint to the ends of the earth, he is translating into the language of dreams the very essence of Francis's preaching.

The first missions, when the brothers were sent out two by two like the apostles, also experienced failures and moments of discouragement which our sources tone down without completely disguising. In fact the objectives seem too asymmetrical: was it ever possible that Francis, the recognized leader, apparently showing little courage, would have chosen to go with his companion only to the neighbouring city of Rieti, just down the road, while sending Giles and Bernard to Galicia, to the distant sanctuary of St James of Compostela, in view of the Atlantic Ocean? One would have thought, rather, that Francis would also have chosen a difficult objective and that he would have been tempted to reach, if unsuccessfully, shores abroad in order to evangelize the infidels, even at the risk of martyrdom (this was a plan which he later pursued quite often). In that case is it not more probable that Rieti, like Spoleto some years earlier, indicates a stop to this ambitious plan, which then had to be rethought? Since at that time the gospel mission could not be recounted as a failure, far less a failure on the part of the leader, there was nothing for it but to terminate the mission by a supernatural intervention. 'Soon after' his departure, we are told, Francis felt an irresistible desire to see his companions again and returned to the Portiuncula, where he found them miraculously gathered. For us, this miracle seems more like a hasty return from an ill-prepared journey. Similarly, the prophetic discourse that Francis addresses to the companions to encourage them is strangely contradictory:

> We will find now, at the beginning of our life, fruits that are extremely sweet and pleasant to eat; but a little later some that are less sweet and less pleasant will be offered; and lastly, some that are full of bitterness will be given, which we will not be able to eat, for because of the bitterness they will be inedible to all, though they will manifest some external fragrance and beauty. And in truth, as I have told you, the Lord will give us increase unto a great nation. In the end, however, it will so happen just as though a man were to cast his nets into the sea or into some lake and enclose a great number of fishes, and, when he has put them all into his boat, not liking to carry them all because of their great number, he gathers the bigger ones and those that please him into his vessels and throws the rest away.

We get the impression that Francis is losing courage and beginning to see the dangers of his success: many have become Friars Minor not because of a deep commitment to his plan but impelled by a superficial attraction for the brilliant renown of a famous saint and desiring to benefit from his prestige. Did not the increase in the number of brothers weaken the spiritual verve of the first period, introducing oppositions and divisions, and causing losses? As we know, in reality Francis's prophecy is expressing the judgment of Thomas of Celano on the situation in the Order some years after the death of its founder.

However, despite its mistakes and sometimes barren experiences, all in all the little community experienced an intense and happy time: the brothers, each extraordinary in his own way, were united by a great affection, a spirit of charity, an enthusiasm above all for their new life, and by faith in God and in Francis.

There is perhaps no page which renders better the climate of the rising community than this extract from the *Sacrum Commercium*, the *Romance of St Francis with Lady Poverty* – an anonymous text of uncertain date. The life described in it is simple and serene, without excessive penances, attentively benevolent towards the inevitable needs of 'brother body'; indigence is welcomed with joy, since it is willingly accepted, the vehicle of an infinite freedom of spirit which swells dreams and aspirations, making light of every obstacle in the face of the ardent desire to follow Christ. After a long journey, Francis and the companions, together with Lady Poverty, arrive at the place where they usually live; it is almost noon and they immediately prepare some refreshment. When everything is ready, they ask her eagerly to share their meal. But the fine lady, who knows only the rich and regulated life of the monks, first wants to visit the places where she thinks that they pass the day, rigidly divided by the liturgical hours. Here is the response of Lady Poverty to the invitation of the brothers:

'Show me first your oratory, chapter room, and cloister; your refectory, your kitchen, your dormitory and stable; show me your fine chairs, your polished tables, your great houses. I do not see any of these things. I see only that you are cheerful and happy, overflowing with joy, replete with consolation, as though you expect everything will be given to you just at your wish.' They answered, saying:

'Our Lady and our Queen, we, your servants, are tired from our long journey, and you too, coming with us, have suffered not a little. Let us therefore first eat, if it please you, and thus refreshed we will fulfil all your wishes.'

'What you say pleases me,' she replied; 'but now bring water so that we may wash our hands, and towels to dry them.' They very quickly brought a broken earthenware bowl filled with water, for there was not a whole one in that place. And pouring the water over her hands, they looked here and there for a towel. But when they did not find one, one of the brothers gave her the tunic with which he was clothed so that she could dry her hands with it. Taking it with thanks, she magnified God in her heart because he had placed her in the midst of such men. They then took her to the place where the table was prepared. When she had come there, she looked about, and, seeing nothing but three or four crusts of barley or bran bread placed upon the grass, she was greatly astonished and said to herself: 'Who has ever seen such things in the ancient generations? Blessed are you, Lord God, whose is the care of all things; for your power is at hand when you will; by such works you have taught your people to be pleasing to you.' They sat down and together they gave thanks to God for all his gifts.

Lady Poverty then commanded the cooked food to be brought in dishes. And behold, a single dish was brought filled with cold water, that they might all dip their bread in it; there was neither an abundance of dishes there nor a variety of cooked foods. She asked that she be given at least some uncooked, sweet-smelling herbs. But since they had no gardener and knew nothing of a garden, they gathered some wild herbs in the woods and set these before her. She said: 'Bring me a little salt to season the herbs, for they are bitter.' And they said: 'Wait, Lady, and we will go to the city and get some for you, if some one will give it to us.'

'Well, then,' she said, 'give me a knife so I may cut off what is superfluous and that I may cut the bread, which is very hard and dry.' 'Lady,' they said to her, 'we have no blacksmith to make swords for us. For now, just use your teeth in place of a knife and later we will get one for you.'

'And do you have a little wine?' she asked. But they answered and said: 'Lady, we do not have any wine, for the chief thing for man's life is water and bread, and it is not good for you to drink wine, for the spouse of Christ must shun wine like poison.'

But after they had been more satisfied from the glory of such great want than they would have been from an abundance of all things, they blessed the Lord in whose eyes they had found such grace; and they led Lady Poverty to the place where she might rest, since she was tired. There she lay down in her total nothingness upon the bare ground. She also begged a cushion for her head. Immediately they brought a stone and placed it under her head. She, indeed, slept a most peaceful and sober sleep. Then she quickly arose and asked to be shown the cloister. Taking her to a certain hill, they showed her the whole world, as far as she could see, and said: 'This, Lady, is our cloister.'

The time is around 1209 or 1210. The brothers are now

more numerous: they have reached the fateful number twelve. Wanting, like the apostles, to pursue the task they have undertaken, to preach and evangelize, Francis and his companions aspired to formal recognition from the authorities. They wanted to leave for distant countries and the good will of Bishop Guido could not protect them outside Assisi. So they set out for Rome. With the agreement of the companions, Francis had set out a rule of life, simply collecting some verses from the Gospels. As the *Testament* recalls: 'The Most High himself made it clear to me that I must lead the life of the gospel. I had this written down briefly and simply and his holiness the Pope confirmed it for me.'

The expedition was carefully prepared. When they arrived in the city, the Romans met the Bishop of Assisi, who in the meantime had arranged a meeting for them with the very influential cardinal John Colonna. The cardinal, who had been a Benedictine at the monastery of St Paul in Rome, in turn tried to convince Francis to choose a form of monastic or eremitical life, but in vain. Finally won over by the zeal and steadfastness of the penitent's project, he offered to present Francis and his group to the pope. The meeting with Innocent III was not easy. It took place in several, sometimes stormy, stages, although the official sources have sought to tone down and mask the oppositions behind a vast array of propitiatory visions. The pontiff and some cardinals found Francis's project strange, very difficult to realize and beyond human strength. But John of St Paul intervened skilfully. 'We must be careful. If we refuse this beggarman's request because it is new or too difficult, we may be sinning against Christ's gospel, because he is only asking us to approve a form of gospel life. Anyone who says that a vow to live according to the perfection of the gospel contains something new or unreasonable or too difficult to be observed, is guilty of blasphemy against Christ, the author of the gospel.'

These hesitations are reported in the very official *Major Life*, prudent to the point of reticence, which St Bonaventure, Minister General of the Order between 1258 and 1274, produced around forty years after Francis's death. The testimony is important, because it shows that despite the passage of time it was impossible to blot out such memories. Furthermore, immediately after this account, Brother Jerome of Ascoli, Bonaventure's successor as general from 1274 to 1279, a relative of Innocent III and future pope under the name of Nicholas IV, adds this postilla to the *Major Life*: 'The Vicar of Christ, lost in deep thought, was in the Lateran palace, walking up and down in a hall known as the Mirror Hall. He knew nothing about the saint, so he sent him away indignantly.' Francis took his leave with all humility and withdrew. But he was recalled the next day by the pope's servants, who found him at 'St Anthony's hospice' near the church of Sts Peter and Marcellinus by the Lateran, where he was lodging with his companions. A dream had changed the pope's mind: he had seen a palm sprouting at the foot of his bed and becoming a magnificent tree, and by divine inspiration he had identified it with this poor man. Perhaps the pontiff also remembered the verse from the Psalm, 'the righteous shall flourish like a palm tree'. Francis certainly cannot have been at all discouraged, since before arriving in Rome he had seen in a dream a majestic tree, vast and strong; suddenly he felt himself lifted up into the air so that he could touch its summit; he even succeeded in bending it down to the ground with one hand. Thomas of Celano notes with satisfaction: 'This is precisely what happened when the Lord Innocent, the highest and most powerful tree in the world, bent with such good will to Francis's prayer.'

The postilla by Jerome of Ascoli gives one greater confidence in the polemical version by the Benedictine Roger of Wendover, which is more detailed. Roger of Wendover was a monk of St Albans, in England, and the historian of his abbey. After Roger's death in 1236 his colleague Matthew Paris continued the *Great Chronicles* and added superb drawings, in his own hand, up to 1259, the date of his own death. According to Roger of Wendover's version: 'When the pope saw [Francis] arrive, when he observed this strange habit, this unattractive face with its untended beard, ruffled hair and tufts sprouting from black nostrils, and finally when he read the brother's proposal, which was so difficult, even impossible to carry out, he treated him with scorn and said to him: "Brother, go and keep the pigs, for it is with them rather than men that you should be compared. Roll in the mire with them, offer them the rule that you have imagined, and go to fulfil your charge to preach among them." At these words Francis bowed his head and immediately went out. He began to look for a herd of pigs and, when he finally found them, rolled in the mire with them until he and his garments were muddy all over, from head to foot. In this state he returned to the consistory to present himself to the pope, saying: "Lord, I have done as you ordered; now, I pray you, grant me what I ask of you." At the sight of him the pope was full of admiration, and at the same time deeply regretted having scorned him. He changed his mind and told him to go and wash and then return. Francis rushed to wash and returned without losing a moment. The pope felt touched with affection for him, granted him what he asked for, and thus conferred on his order, by the privilege of the Roman church, the charge of preaching: then he blessed him and took leave of him.' So Francis began to preach, but did not succeed in moving the hard heart of the Romans. We shall be commenting on the sequel to Roger of Wendover's story later.

According to Thomas of Celano, the pope was not completely convinced by Francis's project and gave him an ambivalent reply. He confirmed the Rule only orally, promising that if in the future he noted real progress and sound behaviour on the part of the small community he would give total approval 'more certainly'. The *Three Companions* and Thomas of Celano in his *Second Life* prefix the last meeting with another day of negotiations, from which two striking elements emerge: a providential dream on the part of the pontiff and the vigorous defence that Francis makes of himself before Innocent III, given in the form of a parable which allows a glimpse of the conflict, though without risking making it too explicit.

This is the parable that Christ had inspired in Francis. A king took as his bride a poor but very beautiful woman who lived in a desert, and by her, to his even greater joy, he had numerous children. When they had grown up and their education was nobly completed, their mother exhorted them to go to the king's court. However, they feared that they would be driven away. She encouraged them: certainly they came from the desert and were the children of an unknown woman, but the king, their father, would welcome them and feed them well, for he would recognize his own features in theirs. And so it was. The king recognized his likeness in them, embraced them and said: 'You are my sons and heirs; do not fear. For if strangers are fed at my table, it is all the more just that I should ensure that those are fed to whom my entire heritage is reserved by right.' And he ordered the woman in the desert to send all his other children to the court to be brought up and provided for there. In the biographer's account this is how Francis and his sons (the Franciscans) see themselves; but we should note that the bride remains in the desert. When Francis had told the parable, the pontiff is said immediately to have recalled that he had had a dream during the night in which he had seen the Lateran basilica about to fall to ruin. A religious, short and of wretched appearance, propped it up to prevent it falling (there is a similar dream in which St Dominic plays the same role: this is a borrowing, first literary and then iconographic, by the Franciscans to the detriment of the Dominicans). Once more the ruin is imminent; when the crucifix of San Damiano had spoken to him, Francis, who had not yet been converted and did not know any of the symbolic language of the church, had not understood the sense of the message: the pontiff needed no clarification. Moreover, whereas in the story about San Damiano the truth of the miracle reported could be doubted because it goes back to Francis alone, with no witnesses, the Lateran dream is beyond suspicion: the sovereign pontiff is its guarantor and confirms not only that the church needs vigorous restoration but that it is necessary for Francis to set to work. Thus it indirectly accredits the episode of the crucifix.

According to Roger of Wendover, Francis finally received official permission to preach, and did so in Rome for some days, but without success. He then bitterly reproached the Romans for their hardness of heart, saying that he would leave the city and, to their confusion, go to proclaim Christ to wild animals and birds. 'He went to the edge of the city where he saw crows, vultures and jackdaws on the ground, gnawing at the carcasses of dead animals, while a multitude of birds of all kinds were flying above them.' He invited them all to listen and was immediately obeyed: 'A circle of all these birds formed around the saint and in total silence, for half a day, they listened to the words of the man of God without moving, their gaze fixed on

Francis's face.' This fact, the Benedictine chronicler again notes, did not escape the Romans, especially as the remarkable spectacle was repeated three days running. Finally, 'the clergy and the people came in large numbers and led the man of God into the city with great veneration'. The monk of St Albans has modelled his story by combining two passages from the Apocalypse: the birds gathered in the ruins of Babylon (18.1–2) and the birds invited by the angel to feast on the corpses of he kings and the powerful (19.7–20). Rome is Babylon the great, whither the birds have come to feast on the bodies of the dead, once great and powerful; for the Romans, the lay people and the clergy, who do not recognize Francis as a great saint and refuse to listen to him, are symbolically dead. Roger projects the prophetic shadow of the imminent end on the city, which he sees as the seat of the corrupt papal Curia.

The account by Thomas of Celano, who does not give a precise date to the miracle of the preaching to the birds, is different. Coming near to Bevagna, Francis saw a great host of birds of all kinds: doves, crows and daws. In mediaeval literature the types of birds often represent different levels of society: for example, the birds of prey often symbolize the lords who use them for hunting; the dove signifies the humble and fervent preacher; the coot the faithful who scorn the vanities of the world. This last is indeed a bird which manages with very little, and since it adopts and feeds chicks whom the eagle has driven away, it is a symbol of disinterested charity. In a fourteenth-century treatise, *Les Livres du roy Modus et de la royne Ratio*, the traditional threefold division of society into those who pray, those who fight and those who till the earth or who at least work with their hands, is presented with the aid of particular categories of birds: the workers in particular are identified by the 'doves, the crows and birds of the field or water fowl'.

This text is later than Thomas of Celano's account, but since the kinds of birds to which Francis addresses his preaching are *precisely* the same, are we not right to suppose that he was basing himself on an already well-established tradition? In that case we must deduce that Francis's sermon is addressed to those who occupy the lowest level of the social pyramid, the manual workers. But the poor, like the peasants among whom they are to be found, are also marginalized, weak, subjected and defenceless; and they too can be represented symbolically by the birds. Francis knew suffering and, filled with an impossible desire, wanted the poor and the birds to be able to assuage their hunger, at least at Christmas.

When Francis writes: 'Also I beg, in the charity which is God, all my brothers, those who preach, those who pray and those who work, both clergy and lay, to be humble in all things', he seems to be taking up the well-known formulation of the tripartite division of society, transposing it into the Order. The warriors, who of course are absent, are replaced by the preachers, who are pledged to win the crowds to the Lord through action; those who pray correspond to the clergy and those who work with the laity. However, the new feature is that there is no longer a church (those who pray) separated from the faithful who feed it (those who work): both are fused into a single group which abolishes the traditional, well-tried model.

The brief preaching which Francis addresses to the birds of Bevagna is a commentary on Christ's exhortation to trust in providence (Luke 12.22–34): 'My brothers, birds, you should praise your Creator very much and always love him; he gave you feathers to clothe you, wings so that you can fly, and whatever else was necessary for you. God made you noble among his creatures, and he gave you a home in the purity of the air; though you neither sow nor reap, he nevertheless protects and governs you without any solicitude on your part.' Addressing the birds, Francis is thinking of all those who live by their work, the poor, but also his own brothers, because they too are poor and are manual workers, and, like the birds, are free to go where they want. Certainly, their life is utterly precarious; they are in need and with no fixed abode, but they are not to be anxious about the morrow and they can trust in providence, which cares for all creatures. The comparison which Francis makes between the brothers and the swallow is explicit: 'Our sister swallow has a capuche like the religious. She is a bird which is humble, which likes to go along the roads to find a few grains. Even if she finds them among the dung, she picks them out and eats them. While flying, she praises the Lord, like the good religious who scorn earthly things and whose life is in heaven. Moreover her clothing, her plumage, is the colour of the earth. Thus she gives a good example to the religious, who must not wear garments of a striking and exotic colour, but of a dull colour like the earth.'

Matthew Paris knew Thomas of Celano's *First Life*, in particular the list of the species called together and the appeal of the future saint to the birds to listen to him. He illustrated the text of the *Chronicles* with a drawing and some captions which seemed to him to fit Thomas's version. Roger of Wendover had not reported the text of the sermon, and his successor had to suppose that it was similar to that reported by Thomas of Celano. The title above the drawing is: 'Saint Francis, scorned in Rome, scatters the divine seed of his preaching to the people of the birds.' We see Francis all alone, leaning on a long hermit's staff; at the level of his face, as in strip cartoons, a scroll says: 'Greetings, birds! Praise your Creator who feeds you, clothes you with a suitable plumage, you who do not work,

nor spin nor toil, do not sew nor gather grain in your barns.'
At the bottom, on the hillock where the birds are gathered,
a third caption explains: 'This happened when he was
travelling in the valley of Spoleto and [there were] not only
doves, crows and . . . but also vultures and birds of prey.'
Matthew Paris draws the varieties of birds mentioned by
Thomas of Celano, perched on the ground to listen to the
saint; they include a heron or a stork. On the branch of a
tree he also puts a falcon or at any rate a bird of prey, the
types of bird mentioned by Roger of Wendover.

I do not think that Matthew would have made a simple
collage of two contradictory versions, that of Roger and that
of Thomas.

Roger of Wendover recalls that after the three days on
which Francis preached to the birds, the clergy and the
people repented; they remembered the saint who finally
succeeded in touching the hearts of these 'stubborn and
hard-hearted men'. Thomas of Celano, by contrast, does
not say precisely when Francis addressed the birds: was it
during the brothers' journey to Rome, or during their
return to Assisi? The hagiographer keeps to this simple pre-
amble: 'After the arrival of the new brothers of whom we
have spoken, the blessed Francis set out and followed the
valley of Spoleto.' However, on the return from Rome it is
again in the valley of Spoleto that Francis and his followers
stop for a long time, hesitating between persevering in the
eremetical life and dedicating themselves to preaching. This
hesitation contradicts the aim of the journey to Rome,
which was made specifically to ask permission to preach.
That is why it seems to me more logical to suppose that the
stop took place during the way out.

In the memory of the companions and of Francis, the
choice to preach was attached to the memory of an extraordinary event, the preaching to the birds, which, precisely

because it was regarded as a miracle, was also the sign of a decisive turning point: it gave the group the courage and optimism they needed to go to Rome and extend a project discussed by some members of the brotherhood into a form of life for all those who desired to embrace it. However, initially the welcome in Rome did not live up to their hopes; so a second preaching to the birds signalled the new miracle: official approval, permission to preach, a popular following. Perhaps the picture of events which Roger of Wendover sketches out is largely governed by the very polemical view that he always takes of the milieu in Rome. At all events, as Matthew Paris clearly indicates when reporting the words addressed to the birds, Francis's message in Rome was probably a message of love, even more open that the sermon developed on the way out, since he is now addressing everyone. Francis, who preached to creatures devoid of reason and wanted to convert the infidels rather than exterminate them, also wanted to speak to the powerful and the hard-hearted clergy, categories of which, according to *Les Livres du roi Modus et de la royne Ratio*, the birds of prey are a transparent symbol.

I now want to emphasize a rather strange detail. In pictures, Francis, who spent his life preaching, never faces a human public but always one of birds; and in a number of these pictures we can clearly recognize water birds, herons and storks. and also birds of prey, to testify to the precise meaning of the preaching. We are right to understand this substitute of a flock of birds for a human crowd as a genuine criticism; it is a good representation of the malaise of the church when faced with a very remarkable religious who still very much resembles a lay person. At this time the church was vigorously rejecting the request of lay people for the right to preach, alleging that only the clergy were capable of performing this delicate task, which consists in explaining the holy scriptures in depth. For a lay person, to formulate such a request was already a risk, since it was readily judged a manifest proof of heresy.

Spreading the word of the gospel everywhere and proclaiming it even to creatures devoid of reason: that was Francis's plan. The picture of this stunning miracle makes it visually present. However, at the same time it diminishes its audacity: the saint's everyday encounter with other people is masked by the only encounter which is allowed him, with a flock of birds. In his *Major Life*, Bonaventure, concerned to shield the saint from all criticism, states that Innocent III approved the rule orally and granted each of the twelve brothers a small tonsure to indicate primarily that they were clergy; as such, they were authorized to preach freely. However, Francis never allowed himself to preach without prior authorization from the bishop or the priests of the churches in which he gave his sermons. He asked the brothers to do the same, not only so that they did not contravene the virtues of humility and peace, but also because he thought that they would be more effective if they did not provoke jealousy. Here are his words as recorded in the *Mirror of Perfection*:

We have been sent to help the clergy in the salvation of souls, so that we may supply whatever is lacking in them. But men will not be rewarded according to their office, but their work. Remember, my brothers, that the winning of souls is what pleases God most, and we can do this better by working with the clergy than in opposition. But if they obstruct the salvation of the people, vengeance belongs to God, and he will punish them in his own time. So obey your superiors, and let there be no wrongful jealousy on your part. If you are sons of peace, you will win both clergy and people, and this will be more pleasing to God than if you were to win the people alone and alienate the clergy.

Francis's friendships with women, which only fleeting appearances allow us to glimpse, incurred even greater criticism. This particularly applied to his relations with Clare. In the first biography of the saint, Thomas of Celano touched on the subject delicately, speaking of Clare as though by association of ideas; first of all in connection with San Damiano, and then with the saint's funeral. However, Clare was still alive when Thomas was writing, and it is easy to imagine his embarrassment, which he does not manage to disguise completely and which makes him gloss over events relating to her. Bonaventure is content with a hasty allusion, although Clare had been recognized as a saint for around ten years. Now we would have expected a long account of her, since this recent canonization, dating from 1255, had increased the glory of the Order.

Where Francis is concerned, nothing can be forecast and nothing is obvious: not even his relations with women, or with the idea of woman which was spread by the church to feed the collective imagination. The cornerstone of this view was the Genesis story of the sin of Adam and Eve; above all the sin of Eve, to whom the church fathers attached the greater blame. Thus from St Jerome onwards, the evocation of Eve was inevitably followed by a list of other perverse tendencies of women.

Francis follows the gospel, which does not treat men and women differently: Christ's message is for the whole of humankind, without distinction of gender. And it was the gospel which Francis wanted to make known, the gospel to which he wanted to give life. For Francis, God did not create man and woman, endowed with distinct merits and faults. God created only the human being; it was a matter of

1. Dominico Ghirlandaio (1449–1494), fresco, *The Approval of the Rule of the Order by Honorius III*, 1483–1486. Florence, Church of the Holy Trinity. © Alinari-Giraudon

2. Bonaventura Berlinghieri, 'The Stigmata', detail from St Francis, *Miracles in his Lifetime and After Death*, painting, San Francesco, Pescia.

3. *Cristo sul Monte degli Ulivi* (beginning of the thirteenth century), detail from the bronze door of Benevento Cathedral. (The illustration has been printed in reverse for a better comparison with the illustration above it.)

4. Giotto, *St Francis Receiving the Stigmata* (thirteenth century), painting, Paris, Louvre Museum.

5. Giotto, *St Francis Receiving the Stigmata* (c.1320), fresco, Bardi Chapel, Santa Croce, Florence.

6. Pietro Orimina (?), *St Francis Receiving the Stigmata* (c.1336), painting, Private collection.

chance whether one was a man or a woman. Here is the surprising commentary that he gives in the *Admonitions*:

> God told Adam, 'From every tree of the garden you may eat; but from the tree of the knowledge of good and evil you must not eat.' Adam, then, could eat his fill of all the trees in the garden, and as long as he did not act against obedience, he did not sin. A man eats of the tree that brings knowledge of good when he claims that his good will comes from himself alone and prides himself on the good that God says and does in him. And so, at the devil's prompting and by transgressing God's command, the fruit becomes for him the fruit that brings knowledge of evil, and it is only right that he should pay the penalty.

Eve is not mentioned. For the saint, and without the least misogyny, Adam sums up all humankind. Genesis speaks of the tree of the knowledge of good and evil; Francis speaks of the tree of the Good (the sole Good) as if God had not wanted to, or been able to, create a tree which would also be that of evil; here again we have an interesting case of interpretative criticism. For Francis, it was having wanted to establish his own will and judgment which led Adam to sin along with all his descendants; by contrast, it was because Christ could abandon himself to the will of the Father on the Mount of Olives that he gained salvation for humankind.

The passage in the *Sacrum Commercium* in which Lady Poverty remembers her stay in the earthly paradise seems to me to be the fruit of a quite penetrating meditation on Francis' words. Lady Poverty is Adam's companion, taking the place of an Eve who is never mentioned: 'I was at one time in the paradise of my God, where man went naked; in fact I walked in man and with man in his nakedness through the whole of that most splendid paradise, fearing nothing, doubting nothing and suspecting no evil. It was in my thoughts that I would be with him for ever, for he was created just, good, and wise by the Most High and placed in that most pleasant and most beautiful place. I was rejoicing exceedingly and playing before him all the while, for, possessing nothing, he belonged entirely to God.' Adam gives way to the advice of the devil, who takes the form of a serpent, and then realizes that he has committed a sin. Lady Poverty goes away in tears. God arrives without delay, escorted by an imposing court of angels. Lady Poverty appeals to his clemency and God, in his mercy, says that he will grant forgiveness if he finds the man ready to repent. The variant on the text of Genesis is important and can only be understood with reference to the gospel vision of mercy. But Adam aggravates his fault by refusing to take the least responsibility and accusing all the world, including his own descendants. God pronounces his curse, but 'tempered with pity [a new allusion to future redemption by Christ], and made them garments of skin'. If we did not know the account in the Bible we could not know that this 'them' represents not only Adam but also Eve. Lady Poverty immediately reappears: 'When I saw my companion covered with the skins of the dead, I left him completely, because he had been cast out to multiply his labours that he might become rich.' According to Lady Poverty, even when Constantine allowed the church to operate openly, the beneficial fruit of his action was never seen. Rather, the opposite happened, since when the church took the form of an organized and complex structure, it simultaneously became a power greedy for wealth. The persecution of Lady Poverty ends only at her meeting with her Francis.

To begin with, real women, women of flesh and blood, had been far from the preoccupations of the future saint, who aspired to total freedom and the most absolute precariousness. In his project he never felt the vocation to organize the life of his disciples, not even that of the companions, in any detail. Francis did not formulate a comparable programme for the women, not because he scorned this sex which the church thought to be weaker and the occasion of sin for men, but because, even by making the necessary adjustment, he would have found it difficult to outline a feminine form of the life of perfection which he planned for himself and his companions. Besides, he would have found it even more unimaginable to make women live in the same conditions of perpetual marginality and travelling.

All, both men and women, were fascinated by Francis's preaching. So we can understand how it would have deeply struck Clare, a young woman of noble family, aged eighteen, and also her sister Agnes, her mother Ortolana and other relations who very soon came to share her fervour, her determination and her choice to follow Francis as far as she could. On 18 March 1212, Clare left home by night with a woman friend and went to the Portiuncula. Francis and the brothers were waiting for her. He cut her hair, thus authorizing himself to perform a rite that his very special religious condition made somewhat unorthodox. This gesture marked the beginning of a relationship which was also quite singular. To begin with, precisely because he had no well-defined plan but was animated only by great enthusiasm and real sincerity, his relations with the women, and consequently the relations of the brothers with them, were very informal. At the moment when Thomas of Celano was writing the *First Life* of the saint, what had once been a little community had become a well-structured order, far removed from the fluidity of its beginnings. That explains the evident difficulty of the biographer, which would increase in later sources, in evoking not only in connection with Clare and the sisters of San Damiano but also with other women, situations and patterns of behaviour which were thought too familiar for the time, although they were very innocent. Clare's scant iconographical success, so different from that of the founder, confirms the reticence of the Order in promoting the figure of the saint. Certainly she is present here and there on some miniatures, pictures or occasionally frescoes, but she was never the subject of any great cycle which unfolded the story of her life and her miracles on the walls of a church.

Over the years, the availability of Francis and his followers towards their friend and disciple and her companions inevitably diminished. However, it was never completely broken off. The exceptional personality of this young woman gives her meeting with Francis an unexpected depth, and without doubt he saw in the resolute enthusiasm of her face a clear mirror which reflected his own image, an intense spiritual communion. He had not foreseen it, but he had to occupy himself at length with Clare and her companions. However, this was a responsible care, limited to the women of San Damiano; it did not extend automatically to other groups which flowered well beyond Assisi, encouraged by the example of the future saint. Clare, Francis's 'first little plant', as she liked to call herself, all too soon found herself deprived of her support and her strength. She survived him by twenty-seven years and for the rest of her life struggled desperately to defend this project which the church, over-concerned with principles of prudence and human decency, tried by every means to make her forget. Only three days before Clare's death, Pope Alexander IV officially approved her Rule, granting her by the 'privilege of the most exalted poverty' the right to possess nothing of her own or in common and to live the poverty of Christ, the Virgin and Francis.

5

Greccio and Damietta

On their return from Rome, the brothers stopped on the outskirts of Assisi. They settled for a while at Rivo Torto, then took up permanent residence in the place called the Portiuncula, near a little church dedicated to Mary which Francis had restored previously. This was in fact a little plot of land which the Benedictine monastery of Monte Subasio had 'lent' them along with the minuscule church. Although it, too, was very poor, they had chosen this new abode because the former one could have given rise to property disputes: a peasant, regardless of the fact that the cabin was occupied by the brothers, had moved his donkey into it to make the refuge its stable. Francis preferred to yield.

Between 1209 and 1212 (it is impossible to be more precise), Francis had tried to get to Syria. Had he embarked in 1212, we could suppose that he had decided to set out to take his message of peace in tacit opposition to the hordes of young people who had set out from France and Germany and were crossing Italy to fight in the Holy Land: this was an improvised and tragic crusade, known as the 'Children's Crusade', which was destined never to arrive at its destination. A storm forced Francis to disembark in Dalmatia and make a hazardous return to Ancona. Since neither he nor his companion had any money, the sailors in fact had refused to take them on board; however, the two of them nevertheless managed to embark as stowaways. The crew was very lucky: they would all have perished in a shipwreck or would have died of hunger had not Francis, like Christ, miraculously intervened, first by stilling the storm and then by multiplying their food during the long journey. Some years later, between 1212 and 1214, perhaps when he had reached his thirty-third year, the age of the Redeemer at his death, Francis left for Morocco to preach to the 'Saracens' in the gentleness of the gospel, but ready for martyrdom if necessary, He wanted to 'proclaim the good news to Miramolin' [the Sultan Muhammad ben Nasser] and the others of his religion'. After the serious defeat at Las Navas de Tolosa, the sultan had been forced to abandon Spain and take refuge in Africa: the loss of this battle struck a decisive blow at the Muslim domination of the Iberian peninsula. Francis's journey was meant as a possible counterpoint in a peaceful key, but it was broken off in Spain, where a serious illness forced the missionary *manqué* to abandon his plan and return.

At the Portiuncula, the number of brothers was growing rapidly. Francis in particular had welcomed into the community a group of nobility and educated men including his future biographer, Thomas of Celano. The number of the disciples began to increase, as did the fame of the preacher, from now on openly invoked as a saint. Numerous miracles began to be attributed to him, even those which the apostles had performed as an infallible sign that their preaching was well founded: driving away the demons, curing the sick and laying on hands.

Meanwhile, in 1215, Innocent III had convened and opened the Fourth Council in the Lateran basilica, in Rome, to complete a new reform of the church and to launch another Crusade to the Holy Land, the Fifth. It is not certain that Francis took part in the sessions or that he met Dominic on this occasion: although their projects were different, the two future saints were trying to find new ways of salvation in strict adherence to the church of Rome. Feeling the need to contain the flood of dissidents and the appearance of movements potentially hostile to the church's teaching authority, this council decreed that no new orders could be founded in the future. At that time Dominic chose for his brothers, who are also called Preachers, the Rule of St Augustine, which the Augustinian Regular Canons had already long adopted, thus disguising the novelty of his project under a semblance of continuity with the past. (The Regular Canons are clergy, usually priests, who lead a common life following a rule and who are attached to the service of a church, most often a cathedral, i.e. the church which contains the *cathedra*, the throne, of the bishop.) By contrast, Francis appealed to the oral approval which the pontiff had given to his Rule, thus emphasizing that the recent prohibition did not concern him. So his Rule was the only new one which came to be added to those in the ancient tradition, of St Basil, St Benedict and St Augustine. It was new because it was recent; but its content was also new, since it was not addressed to monks, priest or canons, but to a mixed community of lay people and clergy. Francis intended it as a way of meeting criticisms and reducing the differences between the pastors and his flock, which was thought so ready to disintegrate, so little inclined to obey.

While the brothers were relatively few, they met twice a year at the Portiuncula: at Pentecost in memory of the apostles and the beginning of their mission, and on St Michael's Day, 29 September. Francis had a special devotion for the archangel who had driven the rebellious angels to the very bottom of hell, the prince of the heavenly hosts entrusted with the charge of presenting souls to God. As a true Christian, the future saint could only envisage one enemy, the devil, and Michael, at the very heart of sanctity, reminded him of his own bellicose youth.

At Pentecost 1217, again at the Portiuncula, a general meeting was held at which it was decided to adopt a more rigorous organization for the brotherhood and a clearer division of tasks. The assembly was rightly being held once a year, since it was too complicated to ask all the brothers, who sometimes came from very distant parts, to travel twice in the same year. Then, noting the need to enlarge and to organize the field of the apostolate, the chapter divided Italy into provinces and sent missions outside the peninsula. Brother Giles, for example, left for Tunisia and Brother Elias for Syria. Francis set out for France in the company of Brother Masseo, but Cardinal Ugolini, who was in Florence to preach the crusade, met him there and managed to convince him to return to Assisi once more. The prelate thought the structure of the Order too fragile to survive long in the absence of its charismatic leader. All in all, the first journeys ended in failure: as I have already said, five brothers who had gone to Morocco were martyred.

The French mission, led by Pacificus, who replaced Francis, achieved its aim, but it was thought to be composed of Cathars, that sect of heretics who were particularly numerous in the city of Albi, and it ended in bloodshed. Giordano da Giano recalls:

On being questioned to discover whether they were Albigensians, the brothers who had come to France replied that they were, not knowing who Albigensians were and being ignorant that they were heretics. In this way they were taken as such. The bishop and the theologians of Paris examined their rule and, seeing that it was taken from the gospel and that it was Catholic, sought advice from Pope Honorius. He declared by letter that the Rule was authentic, that it had been confirmed by the apostolic see, and that the brothers were particularly dear sons of the church of Rome and good Catholics. Thus he freed them from the suspicion of heresy.

Of course they did not arrive at this happy outcome as quickly as the rhythm of the account might suggest; doubt-less days had passed before the questions and answers ended in a reassuring way. The same thing happened in Germany, to which a group of sixty brothers went. Here, again, is what Giordano da Giano says:

> Around sixty brothers were sent to Germany with Brother John of Penna, perhaps even more. They did not know German. When they got to Germany they were asked if they wanted lodgings, food and other such things. They replied 'ja' and were well treated. Seeing that when they said 'ja' they were well treated, they thought that this was the answer to every question. Now it happened that someone asked them whether they were heretics and whether they had come for that reason to pervert Germany, as they had already perverted Lombardy. They replied 'ja'. Some were beaten, others imprisoned, others stripped naked, taken to the pillory, mocked and made spectacles of before the people. The brothers, seeing that they could not gather any fruit in Germany, returned to Italy. Consequently Germany obtained the reputation of being such a cruel country to the brothers that they did not dare to return there unless they were driven by a desire for martyrdom.

When once again, in the chapter of 1221, it was asked whether anyone had the intention of going to Germany 'inflamed by the desire for martyrdom, almost ninety brothers arose, offering themselves for death'. Against his will, since he had always prayed God not to allow him to discover the ferocity of the Germans, Giordano found himself part of the group. Desolate not to have known the names of the martyrs of Morocco, he had not wanted to lose the opportunity to know the names of his brothers whom he regarded as the next martyrs. So he approached the group who were departing, asking each one, 'Who are you? Where do you come from?', because if they were martyred he would think it particularly glorious to be able to say, 'I knew this one and that one.' And Brother Elias, despite Giordano's explanation of what he was doing, sent him to Germany.

In Hungary, where the brothers arrived through the support of a local bishop who had paid for them to travel by sea, they were unfortunately attacked by shepherds, 'struck with the sharp points of their sticks' and bitten by dogs which were urged on at them. Giordano da Giano probably received first-hand testimony, because he reports a series of details which are too imaginative to be the fruit of imagination. The scene is tragi-comical: the brothers are amazed at the obstinate silence of the shepherds, who show no sign of wanting to come to any agreement with them; on the contrary, with a black fury, not paying the slightest attention to words or suppliant gestures, they continue to strip the unfortunate missionaries until they are totally naked. Because of these repeated attacks one poor brother was forced to give up his breeches more than a dozen times and finally, to keep them, he could not think of anything better than to provoke the disgust of the predators by soiling them with cow dung.

However, despite some sensational episodes which in time became legendary, the expeditions continued: they were better organized and better prepared. For example, care was taken to add to each group sent out to explore foreign lands some brothers whose mother tongue was that of the country which was their destination. Finally the missions obtained the results hoped for. The community continued to develop. Three thousand brothers according to some sources, five thousand according to others, took part in a meeting at the Portiuncula, probably in 1219: the number may perhaps be exaggerated, but it indicates the degree of success. The collective memory has remembered this gathering under the name of the 'Chapter of the Crowds', because so many mats of straw and cane had to be made for the brothers to rest on. I would also see this as a recollection of the biblical 'festival of booths' which commemorates the annual gathering, in the autumn, of all the tribes of Israel living the desert: for the seven days of the festival they lived in improvised cabins.

Francis resumed his plan to go to the infidels. He embarked at Ancona on 24 June 1219 and arrived in Egypt some months later. He immediately went to Damietta, to the camp of the Crusaders who were besieging the city, and sought to persuade them to stop fighting. Faced with a Christianity in arms which could only think of liberating the holy places by force, and a church which settled conflicts with violence and death, Francis spoke a different and dissonant language, even if, as always, he was inspired to it by the gospel. In Chapter XVI of the *Regula non bullata*, as it were summing up his meditations on the journey to Egypt, he writes:

And so the brothers who are inspired by God to work as missionaries among the Saracens and other unbelievers must get permission to go from their minister, who is their servant. The minister, for his part, should give them permission and raise no objection, if he sees that they are suitable; he will be held to account for it before God, if he is guilty of imprudence in this or any other matter. The brothers who go can conduct themselves among them spiritually in two ways. One way is to avoid quarrels or disputes and be subject to every human creature for God's sake. Another way is to proclaim the word of God openly, when they see that is God's will, calling on their hearers to believe in God almighty, Father, Son, and Holy Spirit, the Creator of all, and in the Son, the Redeemer and Saviour, that they may be baptized and become Christians, because unless a man be born again of water, and the Spirit, he cannot enter the kingdom of God.

So for Francis the effectiveness of the message relates above all to works and example: verbal exhortation only comes second.

An anonymous work in Old French which can be dated to 1229–1231, the *Estoire de l'Eracles empereur et la conqueste de la terre d'outremer*, says that Francis left the Crusaders, whose conduct deeply troubled him, to go to the enemy camp, and that he stayed in Egypt until Damietta was captured by the Franks. After that, disgusted at their behaviour ('he saw evil and sin'), he went to Syria, where he probably rejoined Brother Elias. Thomas of Celano is content with reporting the extraordinary gesture of the saint who 'when battle was raging between Christians and pagans' did not fear to go with a companion to Sultan Malik-al-Kamil in the hope of converting him. He plausibly arrived there during the summer truce of the same year, 1219. The biographer adds his bit of colour, recalling the atmosphere of the persecutions with which the Muslims troubled the first Christian martyrs: the two brothers are said immediately to have been captured and insulted, flogged and threatened with torture by the Saracen sentinels. By contrast, the sultan's welcome is very warm, which makes the first part of the account quite improbable: 'Although he was treated shamefully by many who were quite hostile and hateful towards him, he was nevertheless received very honourably by the sultan. The sultan honoured him as much as he was able, and having given him many gifts, he tried to bend Francis' mind towards the riches of the world. But when he saw that Francis most vigorously despised all these things as so much dung, he was filled with he greatest admiration, and he looked upon him as a man different from all the others. He was deeply moved by his words and he listened to him very willingly.'

All the sources report this benevolent welcome, traces of which can still be found in the earliest iconography. For example it is in the Bardi retable in Santa Croce in Florence, which dates from around 1243. There we see some brothers flanking Francis, who is preaching to the sultan at the centre of an attentive audience whose faces have friendly expressions. In a letter written from Damietta in 1220, just after the capture of the city, Jacques de Vitry also records the courage of Francis, who did not hesitate to go into the enemy army to preach to the Saracens; the sultan is said so to have admired this that he asked his evangelizer personally to bear a petition to God that God would inspire him to choose this religion which the Lord preferred to all others. Jacques de Vitry then goes on to note, almost with dismay and irritation, the avalanche of new members which Francis's preaching had not failed to produce: 'It is again this same order which Colin of England our clerk and two other of our companions have entered, Master Michael and Dom Matthew, to whom I had entrusted the charge of the parish of Sainte Croix. And I had great difficulty in restraining the cantor [John of Cambrai], Henry [the senechal] and some others.'

In the *Major Life* St Bonaventure gives the same information, adding some even more emphatic touches. He is the
only one to report the content of a dialogue between
Francis and Malik-al-Kamil, perhaps passed on by Brother
Illuminatus, one of the saint's companions in Egypt. Francis
issues a challenge to the priests: let them all go together into
the flames; the one who emerges unharmed will demon-
strate by this miracle the truth of his faith, and those who
lose should embrace the victorious religion. Faced with this
proposition the sultan objected that none of his priests
seemed disposed to accept the contest. Malik-al-Kamil 'had
in fact seen one of his priests, an eminent pontiff, though
advanced in age, disappear the moment he heard Francis's
suggestion'. This detail is valuable, since it confirms an
Arab-Muslim source, the epitaph on a tomb still preserved
in Cairo: the very aged Fakhr al Din Farisi, the spiritual
counsellor of sultan Malik-al-Kamil, a man of great
renown, an Egyptian theologian and jurist who 'in the
presence of the sultan, had had a famous adventure with the
Christian monk'. Francis is not mentioned, but it is highly
probable that the 'famous adventure' is an allusion to the
trial by fire.

Faced with the confusion provoked by his words, Francis
then proposed that he alone should go into the fire; however, if we are to believe Bonaventure's version, he seemed
for a moment to envisage defeat. It was not that he doubted
that he was defending the true faith and feared that he
would be punished by God as an impostor, but because he
was very aware that, led on by his great fervour, he had
made an extremely risky suggestion. 'If I am burned,'
Bonaventure makes him say, 'attribute it only to my sins;
but if the power of God protects me, recognize as real God,
the Lord and Saviour of all men, and Christ, power and
wisdom of God!' Francis asked for the dispute to be decided

by a practice in the tradition of chivalry – for example, when a knight went to the aid of a defenceless lady, certain that God would pronounce in his favour against the adversary – but this ordeal was contrary to the will of Christ, who forbade provoking the divine omnipotence in an inconsiderate way. Transported by the devil to the pinnacle of the temple and urged to throw himself off it to prove that he was the Son of God, Christ had replied: 'Again it is written, "You shall not tempt the Lord, your God"' (Matt. 4.7), and on the cross he remained silent at the outrageous invitation of the Jews: '"You who should destroy the temple and build it in three days, save yourself! If you are the Son of God, come down from the cross." So also the chief priests, with the scribe and elders, mocked him, saying, '"He saved others; he cannot save himself. He is the king of Israel; let him come down from the cross, and we will believe him"' (Matt. 27.40–42).

The sultan, 'fearing a popular revolt', did not allow the trial to take place, but admired the saint all the more and honoured him with presents. Francis still delayed for some time in the region, the populations of which he sought to evangelize. However, Bonaventure concludes, seeing that it was to no avail, he was visited by a premonitory dream and returned to Christian lands. He had desired martyrdom and had attained merit equivalent to the death that he desired; God had spared him, for he was reserving an extraordinary privilege for him. This comment by the biographer prepares for the account of the stigmata, which reproduce the torment of Christ on the cross.

So how did this recourse to the flames occur to Francis? It is possible that, having seen how difficult it was to convince people by word alone, since words had to pass through the filter of a translation and be subject to its approximations, he thought that he could attain his goal better by a tangible example which would seize the imagination. That seems to me a plausible explanation, but only a partial one. To understand the 'famous adventure' better, we have to go back to Muhammad.

Some months before his death, the Prophet had received a Christian delegation at Medina to discuss questions of faith. Opinions differed on the problems of the incarnation of God and the divine motherhood of Mary. To settle the dispute, Muhammad proposed an ordeal, i.e. a divine judgment. However, according to the Muslim sources the Christians were terrified by the miracles which began to happen the moment the Prophet began to evoke the divine judgment. So they asked for a truce and preferred a diplomatic compromise. The Christians of Medina had not dared to 'call a curse down on Muhammad, who was a prophet'. By his somewhat unorthodox proposition Francis perhaps wanted to resume this ancient dialogue with Muhammad which the Christians had interrupted. I think above all that he knew how to counter those with whom he was speaking by suggesting a trial which was a part of their culture. Francis's gesture was not a gesture of challenge but one of tolerance, in accord with the gospel principles which he professed. To understand something intrinsically different, in the Middle Ages as now, calls for complete trust in Christ's words, 'Love your neighbour as yourself' – and this is not always easy.

Bonaventure's account seeks in every way to deny that the sultan was well disposed and to reduce Francis's long stay in Egypt, which in fact lasted almost a year, to the single episode of the ordeal; this presentation seems to me to be deliberately tendentious. Giotto, an intelligent interpreter of the *Major Life*, for the first time represents the trial by fire as having really happened – we should remember that this was only a verbal suggestion with no concrete sequel. The painter ignores the preaching to the people, the message of peace. In the frescoes of the upper basilica in Assisi he prefers to depict a dispute between authorities which takes place within the sultan's palace. There we can see the saint triumphant over his adversaries, who are terrified and humiliated, running at the sight of the flickering flames. This new version triumphed: it became the compulsory iconographic model.

Francis then decided to return. It was not a dream which prompted him, nor even the prophecy reported by Giordano da Giano of the Egyptian prophetess who was called 'the tongue which speaks the truth': 'Return, return, because the Order is troubled by the absence of Brother Francis; it is divided and is destroying itself.' He was drawn back by news brought by a particularly brave lay brother who, after crossing the sea on his own initiative, had managed to meet up with the saint to show him the new *Constitutions* drawn up in his absence by the two vicars left in Italy and some other brothers. Francis was then in Acre, in Palestine, having probably visited the holy places.

On the one hand were the words of Christ, on the other the difficulty of translating them into everyday life: that was what was at stake. When he had drawn up norms of life for himself and his companions, Francis's only points of reference had been the gospel and the desire to spread it throughout the world. He was thinking in a dream sequence, when times and places meet in an instant. In his ardent anxiety to obey Christ's command and with the megalomaniac generosity of his youth which had from then on changed direction, he took no account of human rhythms. When Cardinal Ugolino, the future Gregory IX, reproached him for having sent the brothers into distant foreign lands, exposing them to hunger, suffering, sometimes even death, he had not hesitated to reply 'in a great prophetic outburst':

> Lord, do you think and believe that the Lord has sent the brothers for this province alone? Truly I say to you: God has chosen and sent the brothers for the good and salvation of all men in the entire world; they will be received not only in believing countries but also among the infidels. Let them observe what they have promised God and God will give them, both among the infidels and the believing nations, all that they will need.

However, in practice, only a few elect, with particularly exalted spirits, could truly share in Francis's project. The number of brothers had increased, and most of them could not maintain the high standards of the ardent words of their leader: they were simple men who were reassured by a more regulated form of life, one nearer to the well-tried monastic tradition. So they had taken advantage of his absence to rebel against his innovations, which were thought dangerous improvisations. Above all they wanted the dietary regime, the frequency of fasts and abstention from meat or other food, to be fixed once and for all: their model was monastic asceticism and its rigid rhythms, the exact opposite of the gospel flexibility of Francis, who was always more attentive to the spirit than to the letter. The messenger who arrived from Italy found Francis at table, before a fine joint of meat, in flagrant contradiction of the new norms wanted by the brothers. The future saint read the *Constitutions* and then turned to the brother who was at table with him and asked his advice: should they refuse the food that had already been prepared? We can imagine Francis's smile, on being left to take responsibility for the decision: 'So let us eat what has been set before us in conformity with the gospel.'

Unfortunately Giordano da Giano does not give details of the other changes and 'disturbing principles' introduced by the two vicars. He contents himself with recalling two episodes. The anonymous messenger had related that Brother Philip, who had been put in charge of Clare and the poor ladies, 'obtained letters from the Apostolic See, contrary to the wishes of St Francis, who preferred to prevail by humility rather than by the authority of justice. These letters gave him power to defend the women religious and excommunicate their detractors.' Such an initiative had two consequences: on the one hand it implied limitations on the actions of Francis, who was reverential and respectful towards Rome but at the same time anxious not to create or to reinforce bonds and formal dependencies; on the other hand it contradicted one of the basic commandments of the gospel and therefore Francis's programme, 'Love your neighbour as yourself.' Another brother, John of Campello, had acted in the opposite direction, radicalizing the gospel precept and thus transgressing the limits which even Francis had not wanted to cross. John 'gathered together a large number of lepers, men and women, withdrew from the Order and wanted to be the founder of a new institution. He wrote its rule and with his disciples presented it to the Apostolic See to be confirmed.'

Francis got on a ship and disembarked at Venice. However, he did not go to Assisi immediately. Having understood that his strength alone was no longer enough to direct his spiritual family, he had resolved to go to see Pope Honorius III. He had to arrive at a compromise, rethink the Rule and, at the price of some concessions, assure himself of the firm support of the pontiff.

On the outskirts of Bologna he received a first brutal shock. He learned that the brothers in the place regarded the fine house in which they were living as their property.

The saint decided not even to enter the city but to pursue his journey; however, he 'dryly' ordered all the brothers to leave the house immediately – all of them, even the sick brothers – and to do so for ever. Ugolino, who at that time was Bishop of Ostia and papal legate in Lombardy, had to declare publicly that in reality the house was his: this was an expedient to which he would resort again even in Assisi.

When Honorius III had heard Francis's report, he agreed to cancel the innovations of the two vicars and at Francis's request to nominate a representative of the Apostolic See as 'protector, governor and corrector of the brotherhood'. Appeals could be made to him in cases of need or in connection with problems within the Order. Was the request truly spontaneous? At all events, the first protector to be nominated was, rightly, Ugolino. In his second biography, written around 1243, Thomas of Celano puts the designation of the protector in a climate of retrenchment and discouragement. Certainly we do not find any echo of the polemic and tensions which had arisen in Francis's absence and which continued after his return. But it can hardly be by chance that the chronological thread of Francis's life breaks off at this precise moment: at all events the biographer could not present the chronicle of a defeat. Again according to Thomas of Celano, Francis had had a dream before going to the pope: he saw a hen, small and black, which could not protect its chickens under its wings. It is the only dream, a transparent illustration of a fundamental failure, which the future saint both relates and interprets at the same time, as if he were speaking to himself:

'The hen,' he said, 'is I, small as I am in stature and naturally dark, who ought to be attended through innocence of life by dove-like simplicity, which easily wings its way to heaven, as is most rare in this world. The chicks are my brothers, multiplied in number and in grace, whom Francis's strength does not suffice to defend from the disturbances of men and from the contradiction of tongues. I will go, therefore, and I will commend them to the holy Roman church, by the rod of whose power those of ill-will will be struck down and the children of God will enjoy full freedom everywhere to the increase of eternal salvation . . . Under her protection, no evil will befall the Order, nor will the son of Belial pass with impunity over the vineyard of the Lord. Our holy mother herself will emulate the glory of our poverty and will not permit the fame of our humility to be clouded over by the mist of pride. She will keep unbroken in us the bonds of charity and peace, striking the dissenters with her strictest censure. The holy observance of gospel purity will constantly flourish in her sight, and she will not permit the fragrance of their life to vanish even for an hour.'

On his return to Assisi, Francis had discovered another new development. In his absence the council of the commune had had constructed at the Portiuncula a building of cut stones and mortar to replace the daub and wattle cabins which housed the brothers during the General Chapter. On seeing it, Francis hurled himself on to the roof and systematically began to destroy the building. With the help of some faithful companions he threw down the tiles which covered the roof, one after another. The soldiers of the commune put an end to his demolition work, pointing out to him that the building did not belong to the brothers or himself, but to the commune of Assisi. Francis gave way, but not without feeling a great disillusionment at the change which he noted in his family. He also began to suffer seriously from various ailments, of the stomach, the spleen and the liver; his eyesight also deteriorated steadily because of a painful trachoma which he had contracted in the East. At the assembly in autumn 1220 he chose to resign and entrust the guidance of the Order in all practical aspects to his friend Peter Cattanii. Recalling the time of the primitive brotherhood, a brother asked him why he did not oppose the changes and the deviations which were taking place. 'You know how formerly, through the grace of God, the whole Order bloomed in the purity of perfection, how the brothers zealously and fervently observed holy poverty in all things: houses, furniture and clothing . . . Now, for some time this purity and perfection are beginning to change for the worse, and the brothers excuse themselves by saying that numbers run counter to observance.'

Francis, on the pretext of his failing health, replied that he had put the Order in the hands of God: in reality there was no longer a consensus. If the brothers had continued to follow him, it would not have been difficult for him still to guide them, even from his sickbed. Unfortunately, things were not like that: 'My duty, my mandate as superior of the brothers is of a spiritual order because I must repress vices and correct them. But if through my exhortations and my example I can neither suppress nor correct them, I do not wish to become an executioner who punishes and flogs, as the secular arm does. I have confidence in the Lord that they will be punished by invisible enemies . . . Nevertheless, until the day of my death, I will continue to teach my brothers by my example and my life how to walk the road that the Lord showed me and which I in turn showed them, so that they may have no excuse before the Lord and so that later I may not have to give an account before God for them or for myself.' Perhaps this dialogue took place between the sick man and Brother Leo, since this passage is taken from the *Legend of Perugia* and the voice of Leo, the founder's dearest friend, is more present in this account than in any other.

Francis still drew the crowds, but he was no longer the undisputed, enthusiastic leader to whom the companions had entrusted themselves with total confidence. His bad health forced him increasingly to stop travelling on foot. Preaching became difficult for him, so he wrote, or rather dictated, instead. He very soon lost Peter Cattanii, who died at the Portiuncula on 10 March 1221. He was buried there and his modest epitaph can still be read on the outer wall of the church. Brother Elias of Cortona, who was supported by Cardinal Ugolino, succeeded him. Elias tackled the difficult task of reconciling the opposition; this sometimes resulted in differences with Francis, whom he looked after and followed now more as an escort than as the affectionate companion of old. The meetings of the brothers succeeded in reforming the Rule. As Cardinal Ugolino was present at one of them, they asked him to be their ambassador to Francis to persuade him 'to follow the counsels of wise brothers and to allow himself to be guided by them. And they invoked the rules and the teachings of St Benedict, St Augustine and St Bernard.' Once again it is Leo's voice which relates the episode in the *Legend of Perugia*: when he heard the proposal, Francis 'took Ugolino by the hand' in a gesture typical of the courtesy of the romances of chivalry. He led him before the assembly of the brothers, to whom he addressed this vibrant refusal: 'My brothers, my brothers, God called me to walk in the way of humility and showed me the way of simplicity. I do not want to hear any mention of the rule of St Augustine, of St Bernard, or of St Benedict. The Lord has told me that he wanted to make a new fool of me in the world, and God does not want to lead us by by other knowledge than that. God will use your personal knowledge and your wisdom to confound you.'

However, Francis had to yield. He composed a first Rule in 1221 but, as we have remarked, it aroused so many protests that it remained the *Regula non bullata*. He made other attempts, each of which met with rejection: Bonaventure himself admits in the *Major Life* that one of them was deliberately lost by Brother Elias. The climate was tense: the saint withdrew to a mountain to compose another Rule; certain brothers went to the Vicar General, explained to him that they feared a new version so hard that it would be impossible to observed, and asked for Francis to be informed of their decision not to follow the new norm: 'Let him make it for himself, not for us.' Elias did not have the courage to confront the founder face to face, so the whole group of rebels went in force. Francis did not reply directly to the challenge but turned towards Christ, whose voice immediately filled the heavens: 'Francis, nothing in the Rule comes from you; everything in it comes from me. I wish this rule to be observed to the letter, to the letter, to the letter, without gloss, without gloss, without gloss. I am aware of human weakness, but I also know the help I wish to give it. Let those who do not want to observe the rule leave the Order.'

That is what the *Legend of Perugia* reports. It is our only source for the events which followed Francis's resignation, and we can easily recognize Brother Leo's vibrant partiality. The last Rule, which dates from 1223, is a condensation of the previous rules, but with important suppressions which are so many censures. The text finally obtained the assent of Pope Honorius III, and this was not by chance. The majority of the Gospel quotations have been suppressed and the language is dryly legal, without effusiveness or poetry. There is no longer talk of caring for lepers, respecting a rigorous poverty, far less of the right to rebel against unworthy superiors; the prohibition against possessing books is abolished and the recommendation to work with one's hands is very discreet. The desire to go to preach to the Saracens and the infidels, which was taken for granted in the *Regula non bullata*, is now considered the choice of a few elect, directly called by God. We can note another significant inversion relating to the decision to become a brother. In the *Regula non bullata* it was God who inspired in men the desire to become Francis's companions, so that they formed a small chosen company. In the *Regula bullata* this is a possibility offered to all; the divine intervention has disappeared.

Like Christ on the Mount of Olives, Francis began on a long spiritual agony. He withdrew more and more often to hermitages and avoided the company of his brothers, for whom he often had bitter and harsh words. 1223 was the beginning of the period which the biographers call the 'period of the great temptation', a temptation to abandon everything, completely to lose interest in the community and perhaps no longer to trust in God. But there were moments of remission: the grandiose celebration of Christmas in the hermitage of Greccio in 1223 is one of them.

Francis organized a sacred choral presentation which involved the public who came along. Fifteen days before Christmas he summoned a nobleman by the name of John, 'of good reputation and an even better life', on whose affection and devotion he could count, and ordered him to make the preparations for staging his scene: 'I wish to do something that will recall to memory the little child who was born in Bethlehem and set before our bodily eyes in some way the inconveniences of his infant needs, how he lay in a manger, how, with an ox and an ass standing by, he lay upon the hay where he had been placed.' Are we to imagine that the rocks of the mountains were used to evoke the cave, that some natural cavity was enlarged, or that a large cabin was built to hold the crowds of the faithful? For if it was only a matter of finding a bit of hay and putting two animals in place, the space of fifteen days would seem excessive. The ox and the ass do not figure in the Gospel account; they were in fact added by the apocryphal Gospels. Francis, aware of the message of images, thought them indispensable for his sacred theatre.

Thomas of Celano's account describes what seems to be a marvellous living crib:

> The brothers were called from their various places. Men and women of that neighbourhood prepared with glad hearts, according to their means, candles and torches to light up that night that has lighted up all the days and years with its gleaming star . . . The night was lighted up like the day, and it delighted men and beasts. The people came and were filled with new joy over the new mystery. The woods rang with the voices of the crowd and the rocks made answer to their jubilation. The brothers sang, paying their debt of praise to the Lord, and the whole night resounded with their rejoicing. . . . The solemnities of the Mass were celebrated over the manger and the priest experienced a new consolation.

Francis was happy, deeply moved. He put on the vestments of a deacon, sang the Gospel in his beautiful voice and preached in very gentle terms. His words about the little town of Bethlehem and the divine child reduced to poverty moved and enthused those present. So ardent was he that a knight, perhaps the same John, had a vision: 'He saw a little child lying in the manger lifeless, and he saw the holy man of God go up to it and rouse the child as from a deep sleep.' This vision, Thomas of Celano concludes, was truly fitting, for in fact the child Jesus had been sleeping in forgetfulness in the hearts of many until the day when memory of him was revived by his servant Francis and stamped indelibly upon their memories. In the prayer which Francis composed for Christmas vespers, the description of the birth in the manger is followed by a quotation of the praise of the angels, 'Peace on earth to men of good will' (Luke 2.4): Christ has come to bring peace, that peace which men cannot find in the holy places where he was born, the peace which Francis had gone to proclaim, first to the Crusaders and then to the sultan, and which he now wanted to see welcomed by his compatriots, by the brothers, by the church. Now almost at the end of his life, seriously ill, he knew that he would never see again those distant lands towards which he had travelled with so much fervour. But there is nothing negative about his renunciation, and it did not put an end to his dreams of ecumenical evangelization, since it led him to rethink this grandiose plan and to consider it in another way. There are no privileged places nor audiences: the crib at Greccio does away with the need to travel to the Holy Land or to defend it; there is no need to cross the sea to quiver with emotion, or to impose the faith one regards as true with arms and violence. Bethlehem is everywhere, even at Greccio, because above all it must be in people's hearts: *Quasi nova Bethlehem de Greccio facta est*, 'Greccio has become a new Bethlehem'.

Thomas emphasizes the unprecedented joy felt by the faithful and the priest who, by all accounts, had also been incapable of understanding the profound meaning of the mystery that he was in process of celebrating before Francis's sermon illuminated it for him. In the face of the defects of the clergy, the lukewarm faith of Christians forgetful of the divine sacrifice, the child with eyes closed sleeps a sleep close to death. If the infidels have not known Christ, Christians have forgotten him. Francis wears the vestments of a deacon, which gives him authority to preach; at the time of his ordination by the bishop the deacon (who is placed just below the priest in the hierarchy of sacred orders) receives the Gospels as a symbol of his function. Although Francis maintains an attitude of subordination and respect towards the priest, he brings out the inadequacy of the priest, since only his own words make the celebrant and the assembly feel 'a piety never felt before'.

With this episode Thomas of Celano concludes the first part of his biography; the second and third parts, which are very brief, are only about the last two years of Francis's life, the ceremony of his canonization and an account of his miracles. However, the second part is preceded by a brief summary which again begins in the saint's youth: this repetition suggests that initially Thomas had concluded his work with the Greccio episode. Perhaps the date of the canonization was close; perhaps also, the biographer, knowing the doubts which the pontiff had about it, hesitated to add the account of the stigmata.

Be this as it may, the story of Christmas at Greccio plays the role of a triumphant epilogue. The biographer, whose heart openly leans towards the distant heroic times of the community and Francis's holy folly, here takes its revenge. No, it is not Francis who has suffered a defeat; he was not wrong to claim faithfulness to his first project. It was the rebellious brothers who were wrong, those who had yielded to laziness, who abandoned him and betrayed him. It is the brothers of the time of the hagiographer who are wrong, those who demand security, libraries, ease; they are more insensitive and deaf than the priest and faithful of Greccio.

People needed Francis; the charismatic leader and the companions who share his ideals and his life were the new apostles, capable of provoking visions, preaching and reviving faith in the very heart of the clergy. In a *Second Life*, written, as I have remarked, to complete the previous biography, the function which the episode of the manger had assumed in the *First Life*, as an example which authenticates and concludes the work, disappears. This particular Christmas is mentioned only in a single line, as a prologue to the miracle which Francis performed, again at Greccio, when he warded off the hail and tamed a horde of fierce wolves.

In the *Little Flowers*, the theme of the taming of wild animals is developed in the charming and profound episode of the wolf of Gubbio. After a delicious dialogue, based on his words and the wolf's gestures, Francis obtains a peace agreement. But he takes advantage of it to remind the inhabitants of the country that the presumed ferocity of the animal arises out of his condition: he is a carnivore who needs to eat, like human beings. Original sin brought violence and death into the world: it has made men evil and turned some animals, who formerly ate only grass, into carnivores. This very close affinity which Francis established with animals arises out of the keen awareness of a lost harmony, among both human beings and beasts; he attributes human reactions and behaviour to them. So the wolf of Gubbio could very well be the transparent metaphor for a robber Wolf, made fierce by wretchedness and need.

Thomas again evokes the devotion to Christmas in his defence of poverty, a virtue known to few which is nevertheless one of the essential ways to salvation. At the time the biographer is writing, twenty years have passed since Francis's death. In the company of friends who have given him information, Thomas has meditated on the founder, on the emotional nature of his human relationships and, as a result, of his way of imagining the divine relationships, which he conceived of in terms of spiritual kinship, of family. Thomas recalls some memories: Francis 'celebrated Christmas with ineffable joy, saying that it was the feast of feasts, for on this day God became a little child and had sucked milk like all little children. He embraced with great fervour and avidity the images representing the child Jesus; out of compassion he stammered some tender words as children do.' This scene must have taken place in a church where, as Thomas of Celano seems to suggest, Thomas could have found icons of the Madonna suckling the divine new-born child. In his youth it was the regal crucified Christ of San Damiano who had spoken to Francis and shown him his mission. Now it is the saint who, with a fatherly tenderness, kisses an image, a concrete support for his need of direct dialogue with God. And how many Umbrian mystics, following in Francis's footsteps, would have as their favourite object of reflection images alive with emotions and visions! There they would contemplate the humanity of Christ, in the child and in the tortured man, the sorrowful tenderness of the Virgin, the concern of Joseph.

In the Bardi retable, the translation of the Christmas story into images both reinforces and trivializes their meaning in order to aid understanding: the newborn child is put between the ox and the ass in a way which makes it impossible to see whether it is alive or made of clay. The addition destroys the enchantment of Francis's words, though one can see it when reading the Gospel. In the fresco painted by Giotto at Assisi the word of the saint no longer emerges as an important element in the scene. Francis is only one figure among others, who is leaning over in place of Mary to pick up the child in the manger, while the clergy and the crowd are singing in procession, as if to invite us to take part in their choral prayer.

6

The Stigmata: A Discovery,
A Pious Story or An Invention?

Francis died on 4 October 1226. Several days later Brother Elias, then Vicar General of the order, communicated the decease of the founder in a kind of circular letter addressed to all the brothers. In it he also announced the news of the miracle of the stigmata: this is the first official document which deals with the miracle.

'I announce to you a great joy and an unprecedented miracle', he wrote. 'Never before has such a sign been heard of, except in the case of the Son of God, Christ the Lord. Shortly before his death our father and brother appeared to us crucified: his body displayed the five wounds which are truly the stigmata of Christ. His hands and feet were transfixed as it were by the points of the nails, which had pierced the flesh through both parts, leaving scars of the black colour of the nails. His side appeared to have been pierced by a spear thrust and blood often flowed from it.'

The triumphant and assured tone, together with the deliberate ambiguity of the terms, chosen with great care, are indications of Elias's skill in announcing incredible news which was in fact to come up against tenacious resistance. At the same time it is clear that he was quite aware that he was speaking of a real discovery, something unknown to all the other brothers. When he makes these wounds 'the five wounds *which are truly* the stigmata of Christ' he is forcing the meaning of the event with some confidence.

To discuss the stigmata today is to refer to a known phenomenon, even if it remains unusual. However, at the time of Francis the fact was incredible. Basically, Elias was arguing that a human being had come to be like God; that his flesh, destined for corruption, had become that of Christ. No other saint before Francis was stigmatized. Some rare individuals, of whom traces have been found in the records of proceedings during the twelfth century and the beginning of the thirteenth century, had inflicted the wounds of the cross on themselves without any claim to divine intervention, and they had been punished extremely severely by the church, which thought it a very serious error even to have dared to compare oneself with Christ in this way.

Elias did not wait for the pontiff to pronounce on the miracles of Francis, and the stigmata in particular, after hearing the commission of cardinals explicitly nominated for this purpose. In doing this was he acting in good faith or did he also hope to establish *a priori* the truth of the stigmata by this hasty revelation, counting on the effect of the news accustoming people to the miracle? At all events, he could not be unaware that the divulgence of the miracle would immediately enhance the prestige of the founder and the whole of the Franciscan Order, and also his own. At this moment he was only officially the leader of the brothers. Francis's death, Elias writes, is an 'immense loss for all, but a particular loss for me. He has left me surrounded with darkness, assailed with many cares and weighed down by innumerable torments.' His fears were confirmed some months later: at the chapter held at Assisi on 30 May 1227: Giovanni Parenti was chosen Minister General of the Order rather than him.

This letter did not allow Elias to attain his goal immediately: neither the cardinals who took part in the process of canonization, nor Pope Gregory IX, the ex-cardinal Ugolini, believed in them. The bull by which Francis was proclaimed a saint does not contain *any* allusion to the stigmata, though the recognition of such a astounding miracle would vastly have facilitated the canonization, which took place only two years after Francis's death.

It was necessary to wait another forty years before St Bonaventure risked admitting in his 'definitive' biography the profound perplexity of Gregory IX, inserting the account of a dream which the pontiff had had before Francis's canonization, 'at the time when, at the bottom of his heart, he was still nurturing doubts about the wound in the side'. It is not by chance that this particular wound posed serious difficulties for the pope: according to the Gospel of John (19.37), only the spear-thrust 'fulfilled' scripture by revealing the Messiah in the crucified man. Thus when Elias asserted that Francis's corpse showed not only the holes in the hands and feet but also a wound in the side, it meant that he was not claiming just that Francis had been pierced by the nails of the cross, but also that the saint had, in a certain sense, become like Christ.

According to Bonaventure's account, in his sleep the pontiff had seen the saint appear, his face somewhat hard; Francis had reproached him and told him to get a glass and catch the blood which was streaming from his side. This vision changed the pope's mind and won him over; from that moment Gregory IX 'was so devoted to the stigmata and so eager in his conviction that he could never allow anyone to call these wonderful signs into doubt'. If Bonaventure has not invented the whole episode, he clearly dates it wrongly, since far from disappearing *before* the canonization, Gregory IX's uncertainties lasted for many

years. Among the painters, Giotto was the first to accredit
the dream related by Bonaventure, inserting it into the
great cycle of frescoes with which he illustrated Francis's
life in the upper basilica of Assisi. However, he did not put
it *before* the canonization but immediately *afterwards*, restoring to some degree the precise historical sequence of events,
at least as far as the doubts of the pontiff about this unprecedented miracle were concerned. Again Bonaventure recalls
that at the moment of dying Francis wanted to be stretched
out naked on the earth, but that he was careful to cover the
wound on his right side with his left hand. The Gospel of
John does not specify on which side Christ was pierced.
However, in the iconographic tradition Christ is always
represented as being wounded on the right side and never
on the side of the heart, to dispel any idea that the
Redeemer could have been killed by the soldier's spear-
thrust. St John also reports that the crucified men could not
remain on the cross on the day of the Passover; moreover,
to hasten the end of the two thieves who were still alive on
the eve of that day, their legs were broken. The Redeemer
was spared because he had already died; the spear-thrust
was merely the gratuitous gesture, out of scorn or scruple,
of a zealous official. Christ could no longer have been alive,
so that the second prophecy, 'Not a bone of him shall be
broken', could be fulfilled.

In Bonaventure's account, the marks which the dying
Francis bears on his hands and feet can be perfectly open to
view, the modesty of the saint veiling simply the wound in
the side. When the stripped body was finally exposed to the
sight of all, it was again the wound in the side which caught
Bonaventure's attention: 'The wound in his side *which was
not the result of any human action* could be seen clearly, just
like the wound in our Saviour's side, which gave birth to the
mystery of redemption and human rebirth.' Thus in 1263,

around forty years after the death of the founder, the need was still felt to repeat that the wound in the side was visible only on Francis' corpse, and then with many subtle distinctions. We may note that on this crucial question the biographer retreats behind the authority of Alexander IV, the pope of the day, copying word for word a long passage from the bull *Benigna operatio* of 29 October 1255.

But let us return to Gregory IX, who, as I remarked, did not change his view on the miracle of the stigmata so easily: it took him ten years. However, he ultimately changed his mind: perhaps he was sincerely convinced by the outbreak of miracles performed by the intercession of St Francis; perhaps he was also (and the two reasons are not mutually exclusive) influenced by the heightened conflict with Frederick II. In it the Curia had been forced to leave Rome, an absence which lasted almost without a break from 1230 to 1235. Here the permanent political instability prompted him to seek allies. The canonizations of St Antony at Padua in 1232 and St Dominic at Bologna in 1234 gave the mendicant orders, the Franciscans and the Dominicans, more support, more power and more effectiveness. However, the two Orders, which were both expanding strongly, were also rivals. And it was the Dominicans who fed the doubts about the truth of the miracle of the stigmata. Official recognition of the event became necessary, both to put an end to a rivalry which was more untimely than ever, and to remove the suspicions which weakened the reputation of the Friars Minor. It must also be added that in the course of time the Franciscans had proved to be a fundamental auxiliary to the church, which was finding it very difficult to contain the desire for more intensive and more active participation in the religious life which was being expressed by a society in profound change.

So the miracle of the stigmata was supported by the

Roman authorities, even if many people, including the painters and certain members of the clergy, for a long time refused to believe in them. In 1237, in three bulls all promulgated on 11 April of that year, Gregory IX mentions the stigmata for the first time and affirms their truth: one of these bulls is specifically addressed to Dominican priors and provincials! From then until 1291 we can count nine bulls addressed to sceptics, who are severely admonished and condemned. The opposition came from different directions: above all from the secular clergy who feared the competition of a new and dynamic Order like that of the Friars Minor. The priests had a great fear of seeing the numbers of their flocks decreasing: in the long term would the faithful not prefer the churches of the Franciscans to make their confessions in, to go to mass in, to hear sermons in and to be buried in? And would not the brothers benefit from their gifts, and inherit their goods and properties? As we have seen, the Dominicans proved equally hostile to Francis's stigmata, out of jealousy; they embarked on a long struggle to deprive the Friars Minor of such an exclusive privilege, vaunting the invisible stigmata of their saint, Catherine of Siena. Even some Franciscans who still doubted could be found in the ranks of the detractors. As for the painters, they refused to depict the stigmata, and if they ventured to do so, the marks were very often effaced by unknown faithful. The miracles involving pictures in which the sacred wounds appear and disappear are a further indication of the unease. 'This Francis has become a new God!', exclaimed the monk Leonardo Mattioli of Foligno in fury in 1361, 140 years after the saint's death, on being condemned for having denied the reality of the stigmata. So doubt about the truth of the five wounds was long and tenacious: many people thought them more a blasphemy against Christ than a miracle. The fact that the dream of Gregory IX was depicted at Assisi in particular at the end of the thirteenth century, in other words that the need was felt to take the pontiff as a witness who guaranteed the miracle, shows what great difficulty it had in establishing itself.

In his bold letter Elias had not cited witnesses, nor does he specify when, where, how and why the wounds had been produced, nor who had taken the initiative in likening them to the divine wounds. We owe the first detached and detailed account of the event to Brother Leo, who was also Francis's confessor. On a parchment which contains a double autograph of the saint, the faithful companion adds this commentary in his own hand:

> Two years before his death, blessed Francis was fasting in the place called La Verna, in honour of the blessed Virgin Mother of God and the blessed archangel Michael, from the feast of the Assumption of the Virgin to the feast of St Michael in September. And the hand of the Lord was upon him. After the vision and the words of the seraph and the impression of the stigmata of Christ in his body, he composed the praises written on the other side of this small piece of parchment. He wrote them in his own hand, giving thanks to God for the benefit which had been granted him.

In the *Second Life*, Thomas of Celano tells us that Leo was with Francis on La Verna; Leo too was in the grips of a serious spiritual crisis, perhaps a reflection of the sadness which he saw on his master's face. One day he asked the saint for a written blessing to be a consolation for him, which he could carry on his person always, as a kind of talisman. Francis then took a little piece of parchment made from goat's skin – the relic is still preserved in Assisi in the sacristy of the Sacred Convent. On one side he wrote a few simple and affectionate words and on the other a poem in praise of God. In the long handwritten commentary on this precious double autograph from which I have just quoted, Leo adds that Francis composed it to give thanks for the relief that he had been brought by the vision of the seraph and his conversation with him. The *Legend of Perugia*, an important source which is authoritative because it reflects Leo's authentic contribution, relates the vision of the angel on La Verna but avoids any allusion to the stigmata: it was a beneficial consolation and illumination which allowed Francis to accept the suffering, past, present and future.

In his commentary Leo is quite specific that the marks of the stigmata appeared only *after* Francis had seen and *spoken* with the seraph; he does *not* say that the seraph was the cause of the stigmata and clearly *separates* the two episodes. Moreover, if we turn to the paintings we can see that there are various cases in which neither Francis nor the seraph bear stigmata: the two events, the vision and the stigmata, do *not* coincide; here I would refer to my book *Francesco e l'invenzione delle stimmate*. Leo then connects the sacred marks with a particular episode which took place during the life of the saint, the reassuring appearance and conversation with an angelic being. Elias, by contrast, does not allude either to La Verna or to the appearance of an angel, and he speaks of the stigmata which were visible when the body was laid out only in connection with Francis's death. So the two witnesses do not agree. With the words 'after the impression of the stigmata of Christ on his body', Leo is adapting to Francis the verse from Paul, 'I bear in my body the stigmata of Jesus' (Gal.6.17). *Stigma* is a term which only appears one other time in the Bible, in connection with the prohibition against tattooing one's body as a sign of mourning for a dead person (Lev.19.27). The traditional interpretation is that in using the words 'stigmata' Paul was referring to the scars from the scourgings that he had received for the tenacity with which he had affirmed his faith: he relates the episode in II Cor.11.23–28. However, it has more recently been thought that Paul and his mediaeval commentators used this word to denote the indelible trace left by the sacrament of baptism. For example, in his *Life of Marie d'Oignies*, Jacques de Vitry, a contemporary and enlightened witness to the Franciscan adventure, writes of the excessive penances of this lady: 'Although it is true that we bear in our body the stigmata of Jesus, we know very well that the praise of the King calls for judgment and discernment'; it is clear from the context that here the word 'stigmata' denotes the sign which every Christian bears and not the miraculous privilege enjoyed by a unique person.

We do not know when or in what circumstances Leo wrote down his observations. They were certainly not a memorandum: how could he have forgotten that this was an autograph by the saint and that he himself had asked for this blessing? But by adding his declaration as a postilla, Leo transformed the very nature of the parchment: a personal sign of affection on the part of Francis became a public testimony to the authenticity of the seraph and the stigmata. I think that Leo decided to write on the parchment many years after the stay on La Verna, probably at the time when he parted with the venerable record. I wonder whether the time he chose to compose this commentary for posterity was not the moment when in company with Brother Angelo he decided to put the so-called 'breviary of St Francis' in safe-keeping, entrusting it, between 1257 and 1258, to Benedetta, abbess of the convent of Santa Chiara in Assisi. At the same time Leo could well have handed over the double autograph, after annotating it, so that it would be carefully preserved for ever.

At the time when he was writing the *First Life*, Thomas

of Celano certainly knew Brother Leo's version, and also the letter of Brother Elias. The biographer could not allow himself to neglect either the saint's dearest friend and confessor or the powerful head of the order. But how was he to reconcile two such divergent testimonies? With very skilful adjustments, he relates the miracle of the stigmata twice: first on La Verna and a second time when Francis's body is being laid out:

> The hermitage of La Verna owes its name to the situation which it occupies. Two years before Francis gave his soul back to heaven, while he was living there, he saw in the vision of God a man standing above him, like a seraph with six wings, his hands extended and his feet joined together and fixed to a cross. Two of the wings were extended above his head, two were extended as if for flight, and two were wrapped around the whole body. When the blessed servant of the Most High saw these things, he was filled with the greatest wonder, but he could not understand what this vision should mean. Still, he was filled with happiness and he rejoiced very greatly because of the kind and gracious look with which he saw himself regarded by the seraph, whose beauty was beyond estimation; but the fact that the seraph was fixed to a cross and the sharpness of his suffering filled Francis with fear. And so he arose, if I may so speak, sorrowful and joyful, and joy and grief were in him alternately. Solicitously he thought what this vision could mean, and his soul was in great anxiety to find its meaning. And while he was thus unable to come to any understanding of it and the strangeness of the vision perplexed his heart, the marks of the nails began to appear in his hands and feet, just as he had seen them a little before in the crucified man above him.

His hands and feet seemed to be pierced through the middle by nails, with the heads of the nails appearing in the inner side of the hands and on the upper sides of the feet and their pointed end on the opposite sides. The marks in the hands were round on the inner side, but on the outer side they were elongated; and some small pieces of flesh took on the appearance of the ends of the nails, bent and driven back and rising above the rest of the flesh. In the same way the marks of the nails were impressed upon the feet and raised in a similar way above the rest of the flesh. Furthermore, his right side was as though it had been pierced by a lance and had a wound in it that frequently bled so that his tunic and trousers were very often covered with his sacred blood.

Alas, how few indeed merited to see the wound in his side while this crucified servant of the crucified Lord lived. But happy was Elias who, while the saint lived, merited to see this wound; and no less happy was Rufino, who touched the wound with his own hands [without seeing it].

Then Thomas describes the dead Francis, mourned by his friends.

But an unheard-of joy tempered their grief and the newness of a miracle threw their minds into great amazement. Their mourning was turned to song and their weeping to jubilation. For they had never heard or read in the Scriptures what was set before their eyes, what they could hardly be persuaded to believe if it had not been proved to them by such evident testimony. For in truth there appeared in him a true image of the cross and of the passion of the lamb without blemish, who washed away the sins of the world, for he seemed as though he had been recently taken down from the cross, his hands and feet were pierced as though by nails and his side wounded as though by a lance.

They saw his flesh, which before had been dark, now gleaming with a dazzling whiteness and giving promise of the rewards of the blessed resurrection by reason of its beauty. They saw, finally, that his face was like the face of an angel, as though he were living and not dead; and the rest of his members had taken on the softness and pliability of an innocent child's members. His sinews were not contracted, as they generally are in the dead; his skin had not become hard; his members were not rigid, but they could be turned this way and that, however one wished.

And because he glowed with such wondrous beauty before all who looked upon him and his flesh had become even more white, it was wonderful to see in the middle of his hands and feet, *not indeed the holes made by the nails, but the nails themselves formed out of his flesh* and retaining the blackness of iron, and his right side was red with blood. These signs of martyrdom did not arouse horror in the minds of those who looked upon them, but they gave his body much beauty and grace, just as little black stones do when they are set in a white pavement.

Thomas of Celano emphasizes that in Francis's body there were nails of flesh like the nails which had pierced the flesh of Christ. This is an important feature, since Thomas takes up Elias's phrase, only to contradict it: Elias had spoken of '*holes of nails*' (*puncturae clavorum*), i.e. of wounds produced by the point of a nail. Thomas corrects this and describes the marks by saying that they were 'not indeed the holes made by the nails, but the nails themselves formed out of his flesh' (*non clavorum quidem puncturas, sed ipsos clavos ex eius carne compositos*). This is a vital detail: Thomas wants to emphasize that these were not simply nails of flesh, but that they belonged to Francis's body and came from his very person. Elias had tried to prove precisely the opposite: according to him the wounds had been inflicted by an alien agent, an intervention from outside and therefore divine. By contrast, Thomas is quite precise that the wounds came from within the body of the saint, 'as if he had been crucified *with* Christ on the cross'. Not 'in place of' Christ, but 'as if' he had been with Christ. For the first biographer, Francis does not receive these wounds *from* Christ but *as if* he had been with Christ: Francis's nails of flesh are *a copy* of the Saviour's iron nails, a manifestation of the saint's inner suffering and of an *exclusively* spiritual nature. Again according to Thomas, during Francis's spiritual retreat on the mountain the stigmata had appeared *after* the *silent* vision of the seraph at a distinct moment, to reveal the meaning of the appearance which Francis did not succeed in grasping.

To reconcile Leo's version, which alludes to the conversation with the seraph on La Verna, with that of Elias, which contains the description of the stigmata on Francis's corpse, Thomas of Celano makes the seraph mute and the stigmata the means by which the vision was illuminated. Moreover he was forced to describe the stigmata twice: after the appearance on La Verna and at the saint's funeral. On the one hand, in this way the biographer respected the distinction between the two moments in the story which Leo wanted: the vision of the angelic being and then the appearance of the stigmata. On the other, by postponing the manifestation of the nails of flesh to a later moment which is not specified, he also succeeded in maintaining the probability of Elias's version, which put the discovery of the stigmata at the moment of Francis's death. Had the seraph spoken, it would be incomprehensible why Francis was so preoccupied in deciphering his message. Moreover this silent and beautiful seraph, with a kind and sweet face, but who seemed nailed to the cross, remained an enigmatic and ambiguous figure. This explained both the soothing effect that he had on Francis, as Leo states, and the trouble that the saint would have expressed by the stigmata, which Elias affirms. However, the conversation of Francis with the angel (not with Christ), reported by Leo and passed over in silence by Thomas of Celano, cannot have been easy to eliminate from the saint's story, since a trace of it reappears years later, with Bonaventure, who describes the words of the seraph as *arcana eloquia*. By contrast, the heavenly dialogue was constantly depicted in pictures, to the point when Giotto came to modify radically the pictorial account of the appearance on La Verna.

At the end of his life Francis felt increasingly harassed and stifled by a church anxious to normalize, toning down the project of a Christian life which consisted in practising gospel poverty and love. This was a plan which, had it been truly implemented, would have been revolutionary and dangerous for the structure of the church. Francis also felt misunderstood by a large number of the brothers, and this only increased his discouragement. Their numbers had grown immeasurably and included men of mediocre quality and others with little education, far from the pure ideals of their spiritual leader. Not all were capable of sharing his difficult choices. Like Christ, increasingly alone with the approach of the crucifixion, Francis, aged around forty-four, left for La Verna for a long retreat in solitary contemplation. Only a few of his closest companions accompanied him, those who fully shared in his choices. In this way he hoped to overcome this profound crisis which reduced him almost to despair; he constantly asked for light from God, for a revelation of how his life would end. In fact he found that the darkness into which his soul was plunged only began to dissipate when he understood that he had to entrust the present problems and the future of the order to God's decision, by being ready, as Thomas of Celano writes, 'to see realized in it the merciful will of our Father in heaven': the biographer thinks of the founder as another Christ at the foot of the Mount of Olives. However, from now on certain that he would not rebel, the saint at least wanted to know the end that awaited him. One day, after praying for a long time, he had recourse to the triple enquiry of the Gospels. The book always opened at the same passage or an equivalent one, and Francis's gaze rested 'on the account of the passion of Our Lord Jesus Christ, *but only* on the passage which predicts it'. It is clear that at the time when Thomas was writing this part of the work he already knew the sequel and that he would have to relate the appearance of the seraph and the stigmata. So he deliberately constructs the episode of the threefold opening of the book with quotations from the Gospel according to St Luke which refer to Christ's agony (22.43–45). In the depths of distress the Son asks the Father, 'Remove this cup from me', but he understands that he has to accept all the suffering of an imminent passion. After the vision of the angel the Redeemer feels momentarily strengthened. But soon afterwards he is plunged again into such agony that his sweat turns into drops of blood.

Like him, Francis is on the mountain, here La Verna: he sees the seraph and finds consolation at the moment when he accepts all the sufferings which still await him before death. The agony of Christ is such that it makes him sweat drops of blood; the moment that the vision of the seraph disappears, the memory of the Mount of Olives is so close to Francis that it brings out nails of flesh, copies of the nails of the cross. The reference introduced by Thomas of

Celano is essential; it is the key to understanding the following episode, that of the stigmata, which, according to the biographer, signify *a mental and not a physical* identification of Francis with Christ. The failure of his life and his project were more painful for the saint than the spasms of his devastated body: the pain which he felt from them was more pervasive because it was more lasting and more profound than a torture which at least ended with imminent death.

The miracle of Arles, which is already contained in the first biography by Thomas of Celano, also happened in 1224. When Antony, the other future saint of the Order, was preaching to the brothers assembled in chapter on the theme 'Jesus of Nazareth, king of the Jews', the brother and priest Monaldo, 'of great reputation and even greater sanctity, looking towards the door of the room in which they were assembled, truly saw the blessed Francis raised in the air, his arms extended in the form of a cross, in the act of blessing the brothers. And all those present, feeling filled with the consolation of the Holy Spirit, and the joy which it brought them, found it *quite credible* that their very glorious Father was present there among them.'

Antony's enthralling preaching made the thoughts of the pious brother move towards the one who best followed the example of Christ: so it evoked the image of Francis bound up with the theme of the cross; finally, all the brothers present accepted the appearance, each convinced of its reality. Antony, who inspired Monaldo's vision, exercised a power of suggestion like that of Francis during the Christmas mass at Greccio, when his words were so powerfully evocative that they persuaded a virtuous man that he was present at the awakening of the new-born child, aroused by the saint. In this first biography, after the miracle of the fiery chariot, Thomas of Celano again 'rewards' the pious fervour of the first brothers with an exceptional blessing from Francis, who offers himself to the companions in the form of a vision and no longer under a symbolic veil. However, for Francis the imitation of Christ remains a spiritual imitation, in the realm of the 'as if'.

Bonaventure interpreted the miracle of the stigmata in quite a different way. The importance of the *Major Life* cannot be emphasized too much. To reduce the splits and dissensions which were shaking the order, the author secured a ruling from the General Chapter in Paris in 1266 that this biography would be the only one to hand on the memory of Francis and that it should become the only official version. At the same time the destruction of all the previous Lives was ordered. The operation was carried out successfully: hundreds and hundreds of manuscripts disappeared, and over the centuries the only Francis known was that of Bonaventura and Giotto, his brilliant interpreter. It was not until the end of the nineteenth century that some copies of the condemned biographies were rediscovered, by chance, and historians, finding incredible divergences in dates and content, opened a debate which has still not been concluded.

But to return to the stigmata: Bonaventure wanted to impose a *physical* identification of Francis with the crucified Christ and to evoke Calvary, not the Mount of Olives. He, too, recounts the episode of the threefold opening of the Gospels on La Verna; however, he introduces a slight, albeit decisive, change: the codex no longer opens at the passage which predicts the passion but at the event of the passion itself: 'Three times they fell upon the account of the passion of the Saviour.'

According to Thomas of Celano, after the reading of the Gospel passage, 'the man filled with the Spirit of God understood that it was for him to enter the kingdom of God through many tribulations, many trials, and many struggles'. However, according to Bonaventure, 'Francis understood that he must become like Christ in the distress and the agony of his passion before he left the world.' To be able to feel the sharp pain of the nails tearing a way into his flesh, Francis had to receive an external wound. So he is ready to suffer the wounds of Christ in his flesh, and not just in his soul. Bonaventure then takes up Thomas of Celano's account, or rather accounts, since the first biographer also related the episode of the stigmata in the later Lives. The Minister General sought to improve the story, to make it simpler and more coherent. He composed a very subtle mosaic, using the quotations from the previous texts, to arrive at an account which at first sight is not very far removed from them, but which basically is totally different. In particular, the figure which comes down from heaven in rapid flight, in a cloud of fire, lacks clarity precisely because of the light in which it is bathed. From afar, it looks like a seraph; closer to, it proves to be the Redeemer, nailed to the cross, keeping only the wings from the angelic aspect. Bonaventure has pronounced the key word 'Christ' for the first time, a word which Thomas never allowed himself to use and which he replaced by complicated expressions. Furthermore, Bonaventure makes the appearance of the stigmata coincide with the precise moment when the seraph vanishes: 'As the vision disappeared, it left his heart ablaze with seraphic eagerness and impressed upon his body a marvellous likeness.' It is this phrase which reverses the nature of the miracle: the stigmata are no longer produced by Francis's body but by the celestial apparition. In the *Minor Life*, composed for liturgical purposes, Bonaventure makes use of a perfect comparison: 'so that the likeness of Christ might be impressed upon him like a seal'. It must be added that by dividing the vision neatly into two moments and two figures, the last biographer finally offers painters a version which is easier to illustrate.

By attributing the stigmata to a divine intervention, Bonaventure made this perfection inaccessible: on the one hand Francis remained the saint who ought to be venerated, all the more so since he bore in his flesh the wounds of Christ; but on the other hand, and for the same reason, the brothers were no longer obliged to imitate the founder or to remain faithful to his disturbing words and his project of a Christian life. Francis's sanctity had become inaccessible and inimitable. While continuing to honour the saint with an extreme devotion, the brothers had to adopt other models, to adopt the way of life of other men with simpler and more accommodating virtues. For Bonaventure, this was a political obligation, dictated by the need to put an end to the discord, but it profoundly modified Francis's spiritual heritage.

If we are to understand all the elements of this complex account of the stigmata, it is necessary to discuss one more point: why was it neither the Christ nor some angel which appeared on La Verna, but a complicated figure in which the features of the seraph predominate?

What exactly is a seraph? Seraphs are heavenly beings exclusively present in the Old Testament: in Isaiah's vision they make the temple resound with the praises of the thrice holy Yahweh (Isa.6.2). So seraphs are angels who belong to a time prior to the coming of Christ on earth, and who have no link with the Messiah in Holy Scripture: they manifest the greatness of the Eternal One. But according to the hierarchical organization of the angelic choirs established by Pseudo-Dionysius in his *Celestial Hierarchy* – a Greek work which was translated into Latin and which exerted a profound influence in the West from the ninth century on – the seraphs are the angels who are closest to God: fiery beings because they reflect his ardent charity. In the work of creation in which 'the Word was with God and the word was God' (John 1.1–2), there is a project which is not accomplished on the seventh day: the Redeemer still has the mission to bring sinful men to heaven and to manifest God the Father by making him visible. That is why in Pseudo-Dionysius, but also in the introit of the Third Mass of Christmas, Christ is called the 'angel of great counsel', sent by the Father to his creatures: as angel, Christ is a divine messenger; as man, he can communicate the Father's will to sinful humanity.

Thomas of Celano is the first to attempt the difficult description of the appearance on La Verna and the manifestation of the stigmata. He sketches out a complicated but penetrating image (a heavenly being who is neither totally a seraph nor completely a crucified man), thus forcing himself and subsequent biographers to observe a somewhat inconvenient fidelity to the narrative. According to the first biographer the seraph, who both consoles Francis by his beauty and terrifies him by his appearance as the crucified Christ, represents for the saint the love of the Father Creator who does not abandon the sinful creature; that is why something of the Word who is *then* incarnate and made man *shines through* in the seraph. But I would emphasize that the heavenly vision brings out and exalts the divine component of the Father and consequently the Son, who with the Holy Spirit are all one. In other words, the Word, Isaiah's 'angel of mighty counsel' (9.6), the messenger of the Father, shines out and speaks through the incandescent and immaterial aspect of the seraph, a mirror of the ardent generosity of God. On La Verna, Francis is not absorbed in the contemplation of the different moments of the passion; he is not trying to relive the scourging, the blows, the insults, the pain of the nails or the crown of thorns, as a group of mystics, men and women, were to do after him, particularly attracted by an emotional identification with the physical torture suffered by the body of Christ. Francis's heart is melted and burns in contemplation of the divine love which did not hesitate to sacrifice itself for humanity, meditating on the love of the Father who prefers to lose his Son and send him to his death rather than abandon sinful humankind. Of course Francis was well aware that the Trinity is composed of three equal and distinct persons who are one God; moreover, in speaking of the Father and the Son as though this were a simple relationship within a human family, I am aware that I am not expressing myself with theological rigour; nevertheless I am trying to bring out the aspects of the dogma of the Trinity which Francis's religious devotion emphasized.

On La Verna, Francis is plunged into the darkness of a profound crisis. After a long period of spiritual retreat he finally has an illumination and glimpses the solution: if Christ, who is God, surrendered to the will of the Father, must not he, poor sinful man, do the same thing? La Verna, the seraph, the conversation with the angel – all this can also be seen in that light.

Leo, who collected Francis's confidences, does not say that the crucified Christ spoke with the saint: the evocation of the tortured flesh of the Redeemer would in fact have totally changed the sense of Francis's reflection. Rather, Leo refers to a seraph, who symbolizes the love of God, of God the Father for his creature. On the drawing which he makes of the episode of the stigmata, Matthew Paris depicts a seraph Christ nailed to the cross and writes on it the commentary *magni consilii Angelus*, 'the angel of mighty counsel'. The Benedictine, who clearly grasped the significance of the appearance, interprets the vision as a dream, because Francis is sleeping, relaxed and serene.

Thomas of Celano sees in the seraph a symbol both of spiritual pain and of the ardent love of the Redeemer, who accepted the Father's will on the Mount of Olives. That is why the biographer emphasizes the suffering and love of the seraph, a being who is completely incorporeal, and contents himself with alluding to the crucifixion. By contrast Bonaventure, by explicitly emphasizing the resemblance to the seraph to Christ on the cross, with whom the angel is progressively identified during the narrative, emphasizes the human and physical, not the divine, pain of the Redeemer. That is the necessary prelude to identifying Francis's wounds with the wounds of Christ on the cross.

According to Thomas of Celano, the apparition on La Verna does not take the form of a precise figure to which one would only have to assign the right name to identify it: a saint, the Virgin or Christ. It is an intuition. The hagiographer used all his subtlety and all his penetrating insight to translate a truth which is difficult to express; the result is the description of a complex and contradictory apparition, most unsatisfying if the aim had been to increase the cult and the devotion shown to Francis. By contrast, Bonaventure's account is linear and clear: the brothers could even use it in the liturgy commemorating the founder of their Order, and Giotto had it in mind when he came to represent the episode in accordance with a formula which from then on was destined to become fixed and be immediately recognizable by the faithful. This was indeed Bonaventure's plan, which he succeeded in accomplishing, but in the process the appearance on La Verna undergoes a radical change of meaning.

Francis encountered the seraph only two years before he died; he was thus approaching the end of a short, intense and feverish life.

His condition had got worse. He was covered with sores,

and malaria caused him constant fevers; the trachoma in his eyes which he had contracted in Egypt gained ground; the light troubled him more every day and he often had to hide his whole face under a capuche. As a result of obstinately looking after the lepers he had probably caught their disease, and after a long period of incubation it was beginning to manifest itself. It is possible that the heads of the nails of flesh described by Thomas of Celano were in fact leprous excrescences. Francis's body was decaying; it was covered with with ulcers and often bled. However, his conduct was exemplary, and the edifying power of his patience in the face of spiritual and physical suffering inspired his closest and dearest companions to comparisons of a remarkable kind: it seemed to them that in his turn their great friend was following the way taken by Christ.

Thomas of Celano would certainly have liked to quote some witnesses who had seen the saint's stigmata while he was alive, or to report some revealing piece of dialogue. But his scruples as a historian did not allow him. Perhaps regretfully, the biographer notes that Francis never said that he had received the stigmata and he never uttered this word. On the contrary, the saint firmly rebuked any comparison which went in this direction and was particularly sharp in cutting short any easy extrapolations about the origin of the traces of blood which the companions could see on his tunic. '*Curam habe de facto tuo*', 'Mind your own business!', he said one day to a companion who pestered him with indiscreet questions; that is all that Thomas of Celano ventures to recall in the second biography to accredit the authenticity of the stigmata. In the first version he had been able to cite only a single eyewitness, who was evidently indispensable: Brother Elias.

As well as Brother Elias, Brother Leo was also present at the moment when the saint's body was stripped and prepared for the funeral. According to a confidence received by the Franciscan chronicler Salimbene de Adam, when he saw the naked body, the dear companion of Frances thought that he saw before him 'a crucified man who had just been taken down from the cross'. Leo is careful not to pronounce the word 'Christ'. However, one can imagine that this phrase was an illumination and an extraordinary consolation for Elias. To recognize the stigmata in the wounds of the dead Francis gave him a means of evoking the founder otherwise than as a discouraged, gloomy, tormented man; it became possible to give another meaning to Francis's physical torments, making them a singular and unique privilege granted by God. Elias then decided to liken the wounds which were finally visible to the stigmata and to give the greatest possible publicity to the miracle, transforming the affliction of the brothers over the sorry dead body of Francis into a marvel to be admired.

The companions who saw the life of Christ repeated in Francis through his literal adherence to the message of the gospel had to remember the last days of the saint as a new passion. Some understood it as spiritual suffering, others as a pain that was both spiritual and physical, then, with time, simply physical. As we have seen, in the *First Life*, Thomas of Celano chooses the way of an exclusively spiritual suffering and likens the appearance of the seraph to that of the angel who, on the Mount of Olives, comes to comfort Christ in the depths of despair and solitude.

So on the one hand there is Francis who, on Mount La Verna, succeeds in conquering his despair by sublimating it in the story of the seraph, which he tells to Leo and the very few companions who followed him. On the other hand are all the other brothers who witnessed the rapid physical deterioration of their master and the aggravation of his sadness.

In time the wounds visible on Francis's body were indissolubly fused with the vision on La Verna. But the divergence of the different versions of the episode and the obvious difficulty in narrating it preserve the traces of the difficulties caused by the account: the perception which the brothers had had of Francis's experience had to be reconciled with the meaning that the saint had given to the sudden light that had illuminated him during his stay on the mountain. The majority of the brothers recognized the wounds noted during the funeral ceremony as stigmata; *a posteriori* they explained Francis's sufferings, which had culminated in the time when he had decided to withdraw to La Verna, giving up the companions and preaching. For him, on the contrary, the miracle of La Verna was the dénouement of a terrible spiritual crisis.

In the commentary on the episode on La Verna which he wrote on Francis' double autograph, Leo puts the seraph and his calming influence first: 'After the vision and the words of the seraph and the impression of the stigmata of Christ in his body, [Francis] composed the praises written on the other side of this small piece of parchment. He wrote them in his own hand, giving thanks to God for the benefit which had been granted him.' The stigmata of Christ, which Leo distinguishes carefully from the encounter with the angel, are understood not as the concrete imprint of the vision on the body of Francis, but as a reference to the profound spiritual transformation which took place in him once he had surmounted the difficulties with which he was struggling. By definitively refusing to intervene in the destiny of the Order, the church or the companions, and by living the last moments of his life as he meant to, the saint showed that he had followed the Master to the end, quite consistently. Leo could also apply to his friend the verse from St Paul and write that, having spoken with the angel and finally having succeeded in abandoning himself to God, Francis bore the stigmata of Christ.

As for the representation of the stigmata, the image which primarily comes to mind is that of the wounds of Christ imprinted on the flesh of the saint. Bonaventure has triumphed; he has succeeded in imposing *his* Francis, helped, at the distance of a few decades, by the genius of Giotto. Thanks to a happy iconographic formula, the artist was able to translate, indeed to refine, the conceptions of the last biographer. Before Giotto, although many solutions had been attempted, the iconographic tradition had remained faithful to the idea of spiritual suffering: Francis was always represented in an attitude of prayer, in conversation with the heavenly apparition, either without stigmata and facing the seraph, or with stigmata on his hands and feet, but *never* with his habit torn to show the wound in his side.

Take, for example, the earliest picture that we have which depicts the miracle of La Verna: dated 1235, it is the work of another Bonaventure, the painter Bonaventura Berlinghieri of Lucca, and it can still be seen in the place for which it was intended, the church of St Francis in Pescia. The saint is on his knees, raising his arms in a gesture of invocation. To make it easy to read the image, his hands and his feet already bear the trace of the nails, which are black and not red: it is important to grasp that these are not wounds but nails of flesh, as Thomas of Celano emphasized. The wondrous seraph, enveloped in the cocoon of its wings, has just come down from the celestial sphere. The cross is absent, and only the disposition of the hands and feet, lightly marked with black spots, discreetly alludes to it. The painter, or more precisely the one who commissioned the painting, is reminded of the interpretation by Thomas of Celano, since he has constructed the composition on the model of the traditional representation of Christ on the Mount of Olives: this is clear from a comparison with the panel which illustrates this moment of the passion on the bronze door of the cathedral of Benevento, dating from the beginning of the thirteenth century. In the painting by Bonaventura Berlinghieri, the angel is linked to the saint by a golden river which seems to cut the mountain in two. The beam of light, sometimes replaced by distinct rays, signifies the light of paradise; it is the conventional sign used by mediaeval painters to show the contact between God and human beings. Here it refers to the intimate conversation which is taking place at this moment. The absence of the cross and the indication of the dialogue in process prove to us that Leo's testimony was not forgotten: his version must have continued to circulate by oral tradition or by texts which have not come down to us. So the pictures in particular, especially after the *Major Life* was imposed, obstinately transmit these two details to us. Nevertheless a radical change was to come about. The one who resolutely modified the iconographic chain was an exceptional painter, Giotto.

His main intervention relates to Francis and the seraph. For the first time in the context of La Verna the saint is shown with his habit open and his side torn, so that the wound on the right side is visible. The seraph indisputably takes on the features of Christ and is presented fastened to the cross. Moreover Giotto traces lines in gold to link the two protagonists in the scene. All these changes are visible in the fresco of the upper basilica at Assisi, where the painter and the Order, which commissioned the work, remain faithful to the idea that the stigmata had been produced by Francis's body. However, this innovation of connecting lines which create an immediate relationship between the Christ seraph and the saint already introduces a certain ambiguity. The fidelity to the earliest interpretation can be felt in the choice of the pattern of lines, straight lines which do not cross. They join the right hand of Christ to the left hand of Francis and so on, always with a mirror effect. That signifies that only the saint is depicted as a real being, endowed with a body; the Christ seraph is just an airy, immaterial vision, as if he were the image of the saint in a mirror into which the saint was looking. Giotto repeats the same pattern in the picture in the church of St Francis in Pisa, now in the Louvre Museum, Paris, being content to bring out ever more clearly the features of the crucified Christ and to make the presence of the seraph fade. However, from the fresco in the Bardi chapel of Santa Croce in Florence onwards, the painter makes the lines cross: one line now joins the right hand of Christ to Francis's right hand and so on. Consequently the rays come from Christ, whom from now on one feels as a presence of flesh and bone; and by taking a diagonal course, they penetrate the saint's skin like arrows. However, to disguise the innovation Giotto does not put Francis in front of the apparition but alongside it, as if he were suddenly being forced to turn because of a flash of supernatural light. Thus the spectator finds it difficult to follow the trajectory of the rays, and only with head turned away does one note their change of course.

The definitive version, for example the fresco of Pietro Lorenzetti in the lower basilica of Assisi, shows that the formula invented by Giotto has won the day. Its fortunes are now assured for ever. The stigmata come from Christ; the rays are the colour of *blood* and, like pointed arrows, wound a Francis who is thus divinized and who from now on looks the apparition in the face. Pietro Lorenzetti and all the painters after him also follow Giotto in the detail of the wound in the chest, visible through a tear in his robe, thus

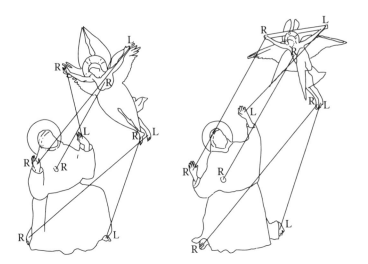

emphasizing in a decisive way this identification of Francis with Christ, which Bonaventure only suggested.

Francis, as Dante wrote, 'on the bare rock between Tiber and Arno, took the ultimate seal from Christ'.

7

Farewell

Francis was exhausted when he returned to Assisi after his stay at La Verna and a brief preaching journey in some regions of Umbria and the Marches. He could no longer bear light, not even the gentle reflection of the candle which accompanied his long nights of sickness and disquiet. He went to live 'for fifty days and more' in the monastery of San Damiano; there he found a small cell where he spent most of his time, taking refuge in the darkness.

Francis felt that he was going to die, but quite clearly did not know when. Now that the physical pain occupied a good deal of his thoughts, he needed simple things, but things which he did not want to give up. He asked for peace and protection because he was weak and suffering. With great freedom of mind, for the moment he renounced the friends with whom he had spent so many years. On the threshold of death he agreed to return to his great woman friend. We do not know how the sisters, and Clare herself, took care of the invalid, and we have no reason to suppose that the sickness justified a sudden familiarity or conversations with the barriers down. On the contrary, a small detail which we shall take into account leads us to believe that the silence and the reserve imposed by the Rule were still observed, in order to preserve the brothers from the dangers and equivocal situations which could result from imprudent visits to the women. However, Clare must have been very comforted by Francis's arrival: the deep spiritual accord which had once existed between the young girl and her master had not diminished with time; on the contrary, it shone out, clear and tranquil.

'Francis's daughters' wanted to profit from his presence. Encouraged by Brother Elias, they insisted that their host should preach. One day when he was feeling better, Francis satisfied their request. He raised his eyes to heaven in a silent prayer. Then he spread ash on the ground, drawing a circle around himself. After that he put the rest on his head and withdrew into a long silence. Finally he recited the *Miserere* and to, general bewilderment, went out. The sisters burst into tears.

Francis had taken leave of them and of life, ready to become ashes again and to return to the earth suggested by the circle traced on the ground. After Adam's sin, God had said to him, 'By the sweat of your brow you will eat bread until you return to the earth from which you were taken' (Gen.3.19). Perhaps Francis also remembered Christ and his silent preaching before the woman taken in adultery: refusing to judge, the Saviour had begun quietly to draw signs in the dust (John 8.11). The saint who preferred John before all other Gospels could have been inspired by this passage: since Adam, has not the earth been the place which receives human sins?

However, in the silence and the darkness of his dimmed eyes, Francis was not listening only to his troubles. As he desired, he had the strength to continue to see the splendour of creation. He did not cease to feel grateful for the gift of such a beautiful world.

One day, happy to have gained the certainty that his sufferings had won him heaven, he continued his meditations aloud: 'Therefore, for his glory, for my consolation, and the edification of my neighbour, I wish to compose a new "Praises of the Lord", for his creatures. These creatures minister to our needs every day; without them we could not live; but through them the human race greatly offends the Creator. Every day we fail to appreciate so great a blessing by not praising as we should the Creator and Dispenser of all these gifts.' He sat down, reflected, and then said, 'Most high, all-powerful, all-good Lord . . .' This is the beginning of the magnificent 'Canticle of the Creatures', one of the first poems to be written not in Latin but in Italian. Francis wrote not only the words but also music to accompany it. Then he sent for brother Pacificus, 'who in the world had been the king of poets and the most courtly master of song', to go through the world with a group of brothers to remind people that Christ had saved the world and to praise God. He gave them precise instructions about how to do this.

Francis could no longer travel and preach by himself. He then devised another way of catching the imagination of the crowd and holding its attention. Those of the brothers who were best at speaking in public first exhorted the audience as usual. Immediately afterwards a chorus of brothers were to sing the Canticle, 'as true jongleurs of God'. 'For,' said Francis, 'who are indeed God's servants if not jongleurs who strive to move men's hearts in order to raise them to joys of the Spirit?'

Francis thought that nature was good and beautiful, that it was a gift generously given to human beings so that they could serve it in order to live. The Canticle, which he had in fact called 'Canticle of Brother Sun', was an indirect response to the sombre Cathar conception of the world, according to which the spirit was stifled by evil and matter. As was his wont, the saint refused to engaged in polemic or to attack anyone with whom he was talking, even if he was a heretic. He hoped to convince by example and by words full of joy and love:

Most high, all-powerful, all-good Lord,
All praise is yours, all glory, all honour
And all blessing.
To you, alone, Most High, do they belong.
No mortal lips are worthy to pronounce your name.
All praise be yours, my Lord, through all that you have made,
And first my Lord Brother Sun,
Who brings the day; and light you give to us through him.
How beautiful is he, how radiant in all his splendour!
Of you, Most High, he bears the likeness.
All praise be yours, my Lord,
Through Sister Moon and Stars;
In the heavens you have made them,
Bright and precious and fair.
All praise be yours, my Lord, through Brother Wind
And Air, and fair and stormy,
All the weather's moods,
By which you cherish all that you have made.
All praise be yours, my Lord, through Sister Water,
So useful, lowly, precious and pure.
All praise be yours, my Lord, through Brother Fire,
Through whom you brighten up the night.
How beautiful is he, how gay, full of power and strength.
All praise be yours, my Lord, through Sister Earth, our mother,
Who feeds us in her sovereignty
And produces various fruits
with coloured flowers and herbs.

The hymn praises the four elements, fire, air, water and earth, which according to mediaeval belief were the essential components of any form of life, including human life. If Francis had been able to look at the miniature which decorates the beginning of the Gospel of John in a manuscript from the middle of the eleventh century, I think that he would have felt that it matched his poetry. Christ is sitting in heaven, but his feet rest on the earth to recall his coming among men and his sacrifice which was to bring salvation; and we see that the idols are falling as John baptizes the first converts. The Son is adored by the angels, in heaven and on earth. At the edge of the sphere unfold, with their respective names, the sea (a man holding a fish), the earth (a woman with a child), air and fire (the first holding in his hands the disc of the moon, the second that of the sun). The opening of the Gospel of John is given at the top of the page: *In principio erat Verbum et Verbum erat apud Deum et Deus erat Verbum* ('In the beginning was the word and the word was with God and the word was God'). Clearly this verse provides an excellent occasion for representing the creation, as is emphasized by the inscription at the centre: *Omnia per ipsum facta sunt et sine ipso factum est nihil* ('All things were made by him and without him was not anything made').

For Francis the sun is the most beautiful, the most beloved of all creatures, because of the light which makes it resemble God, the Sun of Justice. The saint said: 'At sunrise, every man ought to praise God for having created this heavily body which gives light to our eyes during the day; at evening, when night falls, every man ought to praise God for that other creature, our brother fire, which enables our eyes to see clearly in the darkness.' How poignant these words of Francis are, since from now on he was almost blind. They reveal the generosity of his spirit, which was capable of continuing to love the light though not seeing it any longer, and of loving the joy of memory.

Initially the Canticle ended with praise of creation, but Francis added a further strophe when he learned that the bishop and the podestà of Assisi were exchanging excommunications and banishments:

All praise be yours, my Lord,
Through those who grant pardon for love of you;
Through those who endure sickness and trial.
Happy those who endure in peace;
By you, Most High, they will be crowned.

Francis, who had set love of neighbour, peace and concord above all things, felt an unbearable pain at this unleashing of hate. Once again he planned a kind of spectacle: he asked for the bishop, the podestà and the inhabitants of Assisi to gather in the space within the cloisters of the episcopal palace and they came. There his brothers sang the Canticle of Brother Sun, complete with the new strophe on forgiveness. The words, the melody and the circumstances of the composition deeply moved the two opposing sides, who respectively offered their apologies.

Although seriously ill, Francis did not always remain in Assisi. Constrained by the anxious concern of his friends, who could not resign themselves to seeing his condition deteriorate, he decided to make small journeys to undergo various therapies. Brother Elias in particular, but also Cardinal Ugolino, insisted that Francis should submissively accept care. After several refusals the invalid yielded, out of obedience. The doctors applied their remedies, empirical, extremely painful, and as we know, useless. To try to cure the eye disease they summoned a surgeon to the hermitage of Fontecolombo, near Rieti. With a white-hot iron he performed a cauterization in the region between the ears and the temple, of course without an anaesthetic. In this way he hoped to stop the flow of humours which constantly came from the invalid's poor eyes. While the brothers fled, unable to bear the spectacle of an intervention which was so much torture, Francis addressed gentle and affectionate words to brother Fire: he asked for its courtesy and bore the burning calmly.

In April 1226 he had to go to Siena for new treatment. During this stay he was very ill indeed; he spat blood and his companions were certain that he was going to die. They asked him for a memento, a farewell, and Francis, exhausted by the sickness and suffering, dictated a testament in a few words: 'In memory of my blessing and my testament, let them [the brothers] always love and respect one another; let them love and always respect my Lady, holy Poverty; let them always be faithful and submissive to prelates and all the clerics of our holy mother, the church.' For Francis, no value surpassed charitable love and the state of poverty; only in this way could the brothers spontaneously welcome the disinherited, the poor and the lepers, and share their lives with ease and affection, because it was already their own. Finally, the saint was concerned to protect the brothers; he recommends obedience to the church so that they avoid falling into the rigid web of its structure and its precepts.

Francis did not die in Siena. He managed to return to Assisi at the end of 1226 after stops at the hermitage of Le Celle near Cortona, and then at Bagnara. It was probably at Le Celle, during a brief remission, that he dictated a second testament, this time longer. It consists of a few pages, complex and tragic, in which he recapitulates his life and his experience. In them he recalls his total faithfulness to the first rule, to manual work, to the care of lepers, and requires the same respect of brothers. It is as if he were going to begin again from the beginning, as if he could count not only on the brothers whom he was on the point of leaving but also on a long future filled with new plans. He defends the originality of his work, willed by God and not by a church towards which he professes respect, while keeping a serene distance. He declares himself ready to honour all priests, including these who prove unworthy and live in a state of sin, 'because in this world I cannot see the most high Son of God with my own eyes, except for his most holy Body and Blood which they receive and they alone administer to others'. The priests are the only ones who can ensure this 'physical' contact with the deity, of which Francis feels a pressing need, in so doing being very much a man of his time. But at no point does he evoke the church as a guide or a point of reference: 'When God gave me some friars, there was no one to tell me what I should do; but the Most High himself made it clear to me that I must live the live of the gospel. I had this written down briefly and simply and his Holiness the Pope confirmed it for me.' Knowing that death was very near, and fearing the moment when he would no longer be there to fight for and defend his first Rule, he resigned himself to serious compromises so that its spirit should survive, at least in part. Francis had always refused to punish or correct brothers who had abandoned the poverty and simplicity of the beginning since, he said, his authority was based on the gospel and not on power: 'If by my exhortations and my example I cannot repress them or correct them, I do not wish to become an executioner who punishes and scourges, like the secular arm.' But now he is constrained – and who knows with what bitterness – to ordain that a guilty brother is to be handed over by the companions to their superior, who must 'guard him closely day and night like a prisoner in chains, so that he cannot escape his hands' until the sentence follows.

But there was not enough time. This second testament was an official document and, as Francis was well aware, the last: 'The minister general and all the other ministers and custodes are bound in virtue of obedience not to add anything to these words or subtract from them. They should always have this writing with them as well as the Rule and at the chapters they hold, when the Rule is read, they should read these words also. In virtue of obedience, I strictly forbid any of my friars, clerics or lay brothers, to interpret the rule or these words, saying, "This is what they mean!" God inspired me to write the Rule and these words plainly and simply, and so you too must understand them plainly and simply, and live by them, doing good to the last.' As Francis dictates, one can feel his preoccupation increasing: he moves from 'they' to 'you', from a distant future to the immediate present, from brothers to come to his followers, believing that he can count on their affection and their obedience.

It did not turn out like that. Four years after Francis's death and two years after his canonization, the bull *Quo elongati* promulgated by Gregory IX on 28 September 1230 deprived the *Testament* of its status as a binding work which complemented the Rule. The pontiff, ex-cardinal Ugolino, nominated protector of the Order in 1220 and certainly very close to the saint, had sought to tone down violent dissensions within the group by asserting that the brothers were not obliged to observe Francis's last will. Poverty was at the centre of the debates. The brothers were divided on this point between the rigorists, who wanted it to be observed with the utmost strictness, both individually and collectively, and the moderates, who did not exclude the possibility that the Order at least could have possessions. The opposition between the rigorists and their adversaries, the Spirituals and the Conventuals, as they came to be called from the time of Clement V (died 1314), lasted for centuries, bringing its train divisions and heavy costs: life imprisonment, not to mention death, would be the price that certain Franciscans would have to pay for having wanted to defend their ideas.

Francis was not allowed to die in Siena, Le Celle or Bagnara. His body, destined very rapidly to turn into a very precious relic, had to belong to Assisi and rest within its walls, from where it would dispense its miracles to the future crowds of pilgrims who came to pray at Francis's tomb, attracted by his renown and driven by their compulsive hope for comfort.

So the decision was taken to return to Assisi in short stages. The sick man would have liked to see his dear Portiuncula again, but here once more his wish could not be satisfied. The inhabitants of Assisi feared that the brothers could take the body away secretly if Francis died at night, and convey it to another city. Did they fear Perugia and its detested inhabitants? The wretched lodgings of the brothers next to the little church were defenceless and indefensible. Who could rule out a foray by some party or other to seize Francis, alive or dead? In these conditions it was better that the invalid should be lodged in the imperial palace, where vigilant guards could do the rounds all night.

From now on Francis did not leave his bed again; his companions were present, but their impatience did not cease to grow. Even those who loved him sincerely came to forget the friend and his terrible sufferings and saw him only as a body which death along would make extremely valuable. Thus 'a brother, a spiritual man and a saint' one day dared to joke and asked Francis with a smile: 'For how much will you sell your rags to the God? Soon baldacchinos and precious silk will cover this body which is now clad in sacking and rags.'

The saint could not die yet. He often asked his companions, day and night, to sing him the Canticle of Brother Sun, hoping it would bring some relief for his spirit and give him some courage. This singing kept him company, in the silence which enveloped the whole city. The guards, too, Francis told himself, forced to stay awake because of him, would be happy to hear these melodies and these voices.

Elias, on the other hand, was not at all happy with these repeated moves. The dying man was a public figure, already with an aura of sanctity, the founder of the Order. Francis could not be given the freedom to organize his end. How could he have forgotten that this death would soon be described and meditated on, moment by moment? His death had to be edifying, exemplary.

Two years earlier, Elias had had a dream which announced in two years the end of a companion who was already serious ill. This dream had inspired him with the idea that he could stage Francis's last days, and he suggested that Francis should adopt a different form of behaviour, reminding him of his responsibilities. These songs could disconcert, even scandalize, those who were already venerating the dying man as a saint: 'How can he display such great joy when he is going to die? Would it not be better to think of death?' Francis had a last burst of vitality, became irate and replied that he had no need to prepare for his death since well before Elias's dream he had meditated on his own end day and night. At present he felt ready. So there should be no compunction, no tears: 'Brother, leave me in peace! Let me rejoice in the Lord and sing his praises in the midst of my infirmities: by the grace of the Holy Spirit I am so closely united to my Lord that, through his goodness, I can indeed rejoice in the Most High himself.' Then, when the doctor had told him that he really had very little time to live, Francis sent for Brother Angelo and

Brother Leo and asked them to sing him his poem again, to which in the meantime he had added a strophe on death:

All praise be yours, My Lord, through Sister Death
From whose embrace no moral can escape.
Woe to those who die
In mortal sin!
Happy those she finds doing your
Holy will.
The second death can do no harm to them.
Praise and bless my Lord, and give him thanks,
And serve him with great humility.

The two brothers obeyed, and their song rose up, interrupted by tears. Francis, in peace, prepared to embrace the last sister. The Canticle of the Creatures was indeed finished.

Feeling that he was going, the sick man asked to be taken where he had begun his true life in the company of the brothers, to the Portiuncula. Finally his wish was satisfied. After Clare, there was another great woman friend whom he wanted to see again, Giacoma dei Settesoli, a Roman noblewoman, widow of Graziano Frangipani. He had a letter sent, asking her to come immediately. With a view to his imminent funeral she was to bring candles and some grey material, the colour of ashes, to make his shroud. The *Legend of Perugia* notes that Francis wanted to be dressed in grey on his bier, like the Cistercians of France, so that everyone could remember that even a saint is a man, destined like all others to return to dust and ashes. He also asked Giacoma to bring him the little cakes that she had sometimes given him in Rome, frangipani, made of almond, flour and honey.

While the brothers were looking for a messenger to take

the letter, a miracle happened. Giacoma knocked at the door. There was amazement, hesitation. Could she be allowed in when according to the very will of the saint this place was forbidden to women? Certainly, Francis replied, no prohibition applied to Brother Giacoma, as he called her in a familiar way.

Everything then took place in accordance with the pious legend of a saint: the proclamation of the miracle of the stigmata, the tears of Clare and her sisters during the solemn funeral, then burial at San Giorgio and the immediate blossoming of miracles at the tomb, and two years later, in the presence of Pope Gregory IX, the solemn ceremony of canonization. During this time Brother Elias had started on the building of Francis's last abode, a grandiose double basilica whose walls, constructed between the middle of the thirteenth century and the beginning of the fourteenth, were to be entirely covered with frescoes.

All that remains of the Portiuncula is the minuscule church, lost within the gigantic Santa Maria degli Angeli, which has towered above it and swallowed it up. Neither the house in which he lived nor that in which he died, to which the saint's body was transferred in 1230, respected the humble, poor Francis.

Let us remember, rather, in his fresh simplicity, the man smiling at the sight of the woman friend who brought him the little cake he wanted and affectionately gave him courage for his difficult farewell.

Bibliography

The most convenient collection of sources is *St Francis of Assisi, Writings and Early Biographies. An English Omnibus of the Sources for the Life of St Francis*, ed. Marion A. Habig, Franciscan Press, Quincy, Illinois 1991. This binds together in one volume the following works:

The Writings of St Francis, translated by Benen Fahy with introduction and notes by Placid Hermann, Burns and Oates and Franciscan Herald Press, Chicago, 1964.

The First and Second Life of St Francis with Selections from the Treatise on the Miracles of Blessed Francis by Thomas of Celano, translated with introduction and notes by Placid Hermann, Franciscan Herald Press, Chicago 1963.

Major and Minor Life of St Francis with Excerpts from Other Works by St Bonaventure, translation by Benen Fahy made for this volume.

The Legend of the Three Companions, translation by Nesta Robeck first published in *St Francis of Assisi. His Holy Life and Love of Poverty*, Franciscan Herald Press, Chicago 1964.

The Legend of Perugia, translation by Paul Oligny made for this volume.

Mirror of Perfection, translated by Leo Sherley-Price, first published in *St Francis of Assisi: His Life and Writings* as recorded by his contemporaries, Harper Brothers, New York 1959.

The Little Flowers of St Francis, translated by Raphael Brown, Hanover House, Garden City, NY 1958.

Sacrum Commercium, translated with introduction and notes by Placid Hermann, Franciscan Herald Press, Chicago 1963.

See also *Francis and Clare – The Complete Works*, translation and introduction by Regis J.Armstrong OFM Cap and Ignatius C. Brady OFM, Paulist Press 1982.

For the mediaeval works referred to in the text see:

Béroul, *The Romance of Tristan*, translated by Alan S. Fedrick, Penguin Books 1970.

Chrétien de Troyes, *Arthurian Romances*, translated by William W. Kibler and Carleton W. Carroll, Penguin Books 1991.

Those who want to read the Franciscan texts in Latin should consult:

Bonaventurae Legenda major s. Francisci, in *Analecta Franciscana*, Vol. X, Ad Claras Aquas prope Florentiam, Ex Typ. Collegii s. Bonaventurae 1926–1941, 557–652.

Bullarium Franciscanum Romanorum pontificum constitutiones, epistolas, ac diplomata continens . . ., ed. G. I. Sbaraglia (Johannis Hyacinthus Sbaralea), Romae 1759, reprinted Assisi, Porziuncola 1983.

Sancti Patris Francisci Assisiensis *Opuscula*, ed. K. Esser, Coll. S. Bonaventurae, Grottaferrata (Rome) 1978.

Helias *Epistola encyclica de transitu s. Francisci*, in *Analecta Franciscana, Vol.* X, 523–8.

Legenda trium sociorum, critical edition ed. T. Desbonnets, in *Archivum Franciscanum Historicum* LXVII, 1974, 38–144; the text of the *Legenda* is on 89–144.

Les Livres du Roy Modus et de la Royne Ratio, ed. G. Tilander,

Société des Anciennes Textes Français, Paris 1932, Vols. I–II.

Sacrum commercium sancti Francisci cum domina Paupertate, ed. S. Brufani, Edizioni Porziuncola, Assisi 1990.

Scripta Leonis, Rufini et Angeli Sociorum s. Francisci, critical edition and English translation by R. B. Brooke, Clarendon Press, Oxford 1970.

Speculum perfectionis, critical edition ed. P. Sabatier, Manchester University Press 1928.

Testimonia minora saeculi XIII de s.Francisco Assisiensi collecta, ed. L. Leminens, Ad Claras Aquas, Typ. Collegii s. Bonaventurae 1926, Collectanea Philosophico-theologica, vol.III.

Thomae de Celano *Vita prima sancti Francisci*, in *Analecta Franciscana*, Vol. X, 3–117.

Thomae de Celano *Vita secunda s. Francisci*, ibid., 129–268.

Thomae de Celano *Tractatus de miraculis b. Francisci*, ibid., 271–330.

For individual points see:

Chiara Frugoni, *Francesco e l'invenzione delle stimmate. Una storia per immagini e parole fino a Giotto ed a Bonaventura*, Einaudi, Turin 1993.

A. Bartoli Langeli, 'La realtà sociale assisana e il patto del 1210 in Assisi al tempo di san Francesco', *Atti del V convegno internazionale di Studi francescani, Assisi 13–16 ottobre 1977*, Società internazionale di Studi francescani, Assisi 1978, 273–336.

G. Basetti-Sani, *La cristofania della Verna e le stimmate di san Francesco per il mondo musulmano*, Il Segno, Negarine di San Pietro in Cariano (Verona) 1993.

J. Dalarun, *Francesco: un passaggio. Donna e donne negli scritti e nelle leggende di Francesco d'Assisi*, with a postscript by G.Miccoli, Viella, Rome 1994.

F. Gabrieli, 'San Francesco e l'Oriente islamico', in *Espansione del francescanesimo tra Occidente e Oriente nel secolo XIII*, in *Atti del VI convegno internazionale di Studi francescani, Società internazionale di Studi francescani, Assisi 12–14 ottobre 1978*, Assisi 1979, 108–22.

R. Manselli, 'Assisi tra impero e papato', in *Assisi* (above), 349–57.

G. Miccoli, *Francesco d'Assisi, realtà e memoria di un'esperienza cristiana*, Einaudi, Turin 1991.

W. Schenkluhn, *San Francesco in Assisi: Ecclesia Specialis*, Edizioni Biblioteca Francescana, Milan 1994.

M. Vommaro, *I miracoli di san Francesco nella trilogia celanese*, thesis Università di Tor Vergata, Rome 1995.

Mention of these works does not indicate that I accept unconditionally the theses of individual authors, but I acknowledge my debt towards them, since they have given me much to reflect on and have helped in the production of my own work.

Index